Paul's Prison Epistles
- ► **Ephesians**
- ► **Philippians**
- ► **Colossians**
- ► **Philemon**

Study Guides for LIFE

James K. Crews

ISBN-13: 978-1540862464

ISBN-10: 1540862461

BISAC: Religion / Biblical Studies / Paul's Letters

Acknowledgments

Sincere appreciation and gratitude are extended to Diane, my wife of 49 years (and counting). She is my faithful friend and editor who, thankfully, sees life differently than I do. She questions my questions and does what she can to make me look good.

Similar thanks are also due to Liz Briggs, a retired English teacher, who diligently proofreads my writings, resolves my grammatical challenges and encourages me on to greater excellence.

The appreciative reader and I are both indebted to the efforts of these special people. Any confusing or incorrect statements that persist are entirely my responsibility. These few remaining errors are a service of the author to provide meaning and purpose to those who like to find mistakes.

The Translation

Scripture taken from the NEW AMERICAN STANDARD BIBLE®,
Copyright © 1960, 1962, 1963, 1968, 1971, 1972, 1973, 1975, 1977, 1995 by
The Lockman Foundation. Used by permission. (www.Lockman.org)

The New American Standard Bible (NASB) was chosen for *The Study Guides for LIFE* because it is the most accurate, literal translation of the original languages available today. The NASB was translated by a team of over 20 translators from a variety of denominational backgrounds who are conservative Bible scholars with doctorates in biblical languages, theology, or other advanced degrees. The translation by a group of scholars avoids doctrinal biases and viewpoints of any one individual so the translation reflects more accurately what the biblical authors wrote, rather than the opinion of one translator. The translation is as close to the original languages as possible given the constraints of the English language.

In the New Testament, ALL CAPITAL LETTERS indicate a quotation from the Old Testament. Quotations are usually quotes of thoughts and concepts, not verbatim as we might expect. In addition to the difficulties of quoting across the barriers of language and various translations, the authors usually paraphrased what they were quoting. Few people of that time had access to the actual Old Testament manuscripts.

[*Text in brackets*] indicates words that have been inserted by the translators to convey the meaning of the original Greek more accurately. Those specific words are not found in the original texts.

About the Study Guides for LIFE

The Study Guides for LIFE were written to help students discover the truths of the Scriptures for themselves. Whether you are an individual believer wanting more of God or a small group leader, this study guide is designed to help you understand the contents of the Bible and to live according to its teachings.

This volume contains the full text of this book from the New American Standard Bible (1995) divided into convenient paragraphs to facilitate your thinking and group discussions. Each paragraph is followed by various comments and questions to guide you into your personal discoveries of God's Word and to reinforce what He is saying through the teachings of the book you are studying. These additional thoughts are organized into three formats:

1. **FYI:** (*For Your Information*) -- These notes provide additional information to explain the background of the culture or discuss issues that are important to clarify the biblical text.

2. **TQ:** (*Text Question*) -- These are questions which can be answered directly from the Scripture passage. They help focus your attention on significant details in the passage. It would be appropriate to underline the specific phrase in the passage that answers the question. Blank lines are also provided to record your answers.

3. **DQ:** (*Discussion Question*) -- These questions are for more intensive thinking or group discussion and have no "correct" answer. The value of these questions is that they will direct your thinking to the personal application of the text and provide a greater opportunity for God to speak to you regarding cultural issues or your own life.

A few of the discussion questions in *The Study Guides for LIFE* are difficult and may require a more comprehensive understanding of the Scriptures and the plans and purposes of God to answer. If you find a question that seems too difficult, don't be discouraged. Just use it as a reason to seek God and have the Holy Spirit guide you into that truth (John 16:13).

This is not a commentary to provide answers, but a guide to encourage you to achieve greater comprehension of the book. When you are using this study guide for personal study or in a small group setting, spend much time with the biblical text to allow the Spirit of God to instruct and illuminate the passage (John 14:25).

A Word about Small Groups

If you are fortunate enough to lead a small group, recognize that adults learn best when they can discuss the text and share their ideas of how a particular truth affects their lives in practical ways. Greater clarity often arises by the sharing of various perspectives. The small group leader should be a discussion leader, not a lecturer.

The simplest Bible study is to sit with a group of people who take turns reading the text. Pause after each passage to allow the group to share their questions, personal ideas or insights on what was read. The knowledge level of the class is not an issue; the Holy Spirit will become the teacher as discussion takes place in the group. This is an effective study method even among those who know nothing of the contents of the book.

The most effective Bible study is an Inductive Study. To do an inductive study, read the text and ask three questions for each passage being studied.

> **1) What does the passage say?** Rephrase the passage in your own words, then answer such questions as: Who? What? When? Where? Why? How? Like an investigative journalist or a crime scene investigator, carefully discover all the clues that are available in the passage.

> **2) What does the passage mean?** Once you understand clearly what the passage says, interpret its meaning as you would any other piece of literature. God is communicating truth to us through normal human means in a way that is meant to be understood. The Bible was written by 40 different authors over a period of about 1400 years. In its pages you will find several genres of writing, various customs of multiple cultures, figures of speech and both literal and figurative language. Just as we have to understand the meaning of what any person or book says, so we have to interpret the meaning of the Scriptures. It may seem like a daunting task, but simplifying the process is the purpose of this study guide.

> The best rule of interpreting the Bible is this: *If the text makes sense, seek no other sense, lest you end up in nonsense.*

> **3) How can I apply the passage to my own life?** Application takes the language from the conceptual and makes it practical to our

situations. The application is not the meaning of the text, but the way the meaning of the text can be put into action.

> *Knowing is not enough, we must apply.*
> *Willing is not enough, we must do.*
> --- Johann Wolfgang von Goethe

Are you living what you're learning?

You may think that you need to read many chapters a day to understand God's Word—the more the better. The reality is that to understand God, you need to slow down and think carefully about each phrase and word of the Scriptures God has given us. Careful thinking (or meditation) helps you to be receptive to the Holy Spirit's instructions. Answering the questions in the Study Guide will facilitate this process. Don't be in a hurry, but meditate carefully on each word and phrase before going on to the next. (See Joshua 1:8, Psalm 1:1-3, and 119:148.)

Remember the words of Paul as you begin your study:

> *Consider what I say, for the Lord will give you understanding in everything.* --2 Timothy 2:7

Let's begin, shall we?

Table of Contents

Ephesians: A Study Guide for LIFE

Outline and Table of Contents

Background Information

AUTHOR: The Apostle Paul (Ephesians 1:1).

DATE: Paul wrote the epistles or letters to the churches in Ephesus, Philippi and Colossi, and a personal letter to Philemon while he was imprisoned in Rome, about 61 or 62 AD. These four epistles are known as Paul's Prison Epistles. There seem to be no major problems in the churches to prompt these letters. It had been about three years since he had visited these churches so when Tychicus and some of the brethren were returning to Asia Minor, Paul took the opportunity to send letters to the churches along their way (Ephesus, Philippi, Colossi and Laodicea) to encourage them in the faith (Ephesus 6:21-22).

BACKGROUND: Paul's first visit to Ephesus, a city given to the occult (Ephesians 2:2) and the power of satan, is recorded in Acts 18:19-21. During this visit, in the year 53 AD, he spoke briefly in the synagogue and despite their entreaties to stay, he continued on his way to visit and strengthen churches in Caesarea, Antioch and Galatia. He promised to return to Ephesus if God were to will it.

In Acts 19, Luke records that Paul finished his earlier journeys and returned to Ephesus, where he preached in the synagogue for three months until the Jews began to oppose him. Recognizing the danger in continuing his synagogue ministry, he began preaching in the school of Tyrannus for the next two years. He was so effective that Luke reports that "all who lived in Asia heard the word of the Lord, both Jews and Greeks" (Acts 19:10). Paul was performing miracles (Acts 19:11-12) which were drawing people to the Lord in large numbers.

The city of Ephesus had a magnificent temple which held the statue of the goddess Diana, a statue which was reputed to have miraculously fallen from the sky. At the height of Paul's popularity, craftsmen who were making images of Diana for sale realized their market base was quickly being eroded by Paul's teaching (Acts 19:23-28). To stop their losses, they tried to eliminate Paul in a riot. Paul escaped the crowd through the wise counsel of the town clerk. The next day Paul encouraged the disciples and went into Macedonia (Acts 20:1).

There is some evidence that Paul did not write this epistle specifically to the Ephesian church. Paul had labored for three years in Ephesus (Acts 20:31), yet this letter has no personal references to people he must have known in the city. The most workable explanation is that this letter was something like a circular letter that was intended to be shared with several churches. Perhaps it is the letter that was refer-enced in Colossians 4:16 and was originally sent to Laodicea.

A-1   Salutation – Ephesians 1:1-2

Ephesians 1:1-2   *Paul, an apostle of Christ Jesus by the will of God, To the saints who are at Ephesus and [who are] faithful in Christ Jesus:* **2** *Grace to you and peace from God our Father and the Lord Jesus Christ.*

FYI: Begin now to separately identify all references to the Father, the Son and the Holy Spirit in this epistle. Highlighting each name and pro-noun with a different colored pencil for each Person is very effective, but you could also put letters ("F," "J," or "HS") over each reference.

At least one early manuscript has the word "Ephesus" written in dif-ferent hand-writing. This gives evidence to the idea that the letter was actually a circular letter that was written, copied and then distributed to several churches, not just Ephesus.

TQ: ** Who wrote this letter?_____

** To whom was it written?_____

_____

** What is the blessing?_____

_____

** Begin a list of the benefits and advantages we have "in Christ" as shown in this epistle._____

_____

A-2   SIT: Our Position in Christ – Ephesians 1:3-3:21

B-1   The Work of God-the-Father – Ephesians 1:3-2:23

C-1   The Blessings of God – Ephesians 1:3-14

Ephesians 1:3-4b   *Blessed [be] the God and Father of our Lord Jesus Christ, who has blessed us with every spiritual bless-ing in the heavenly [places] in Christ,* **4** *just as He chose us in Him before the foundation of the world, that we would be holy and blameless before Him.*

FYI: Before He began creating this physical universe, God knew mankind would sin and He established the entire plan of salvation to restore all people to Himself. He determined that every person who believed in the sacrifice of His Son on the cross would be forgiven and made holy and blameless in His sight.

TQ: ** What do we learn about God and Christ from this passage?_____
_____

** How has the Father blessed us?_____
_____

** Why did we receive these blessings?_____
_____

** When did we get them?_____
_____

** Where are these blessings found?_____
_____

Ephesians 1:4c-6 *In love* **5** *He predestined us to adoption as sons through Jesus Christ to Himself, according to the kind intention of His will,* **6** *to the praise of the glory of His grace, which He freely bestowed on us in the Beloved.*

FYI: We are born into the kingdom of God, not adopted into it. The adoption as sons is a lifelong process of maturity that is concluded at the return of Christ and the resurrection of our bodies. Believers in Christ have been predestined to become mature and capable sons and daughters in Christ's kingdom. (See Glossary: *Adoption as Sons*.)

TQ: ** What is God's intention and destiny for us?_____
_____

** What was His motivation?_____
_____

** Where do we find grace?_____
_____

Ephesians 1:7-10c *In Him we have redemption through His blood, the forgiveness of our trespasses, according to the riches of His grace* **8** *which He lavished on us. In all wisdom and insight* **9** *He made known to us the mystery of His will, according to His kind intention which He purposed in Him* **10** *with a view to an administration suitable to the fullness of the times, [that is], the summing up* *of all things in Christ, things in the heavens and things on the earth.*

FYI: **Lavished** (Gk. *perisseuo*) – that which comes in abundance, or overflows; something which falls to the lot of one in large measure; to be abundantly furnished with; to be over and above in abundant supply.

Be sure to identify each of the pronouns (Him, He, His) in this and future passages. This section can be particularly difficult if the pronouns aren't clearly identified.

TQ: ** Who is "Him" in verse seven?_____

** What do we have in "Him"?_____

_____

** Who is doing the lavishing?_____

** What did He lavish on us?_____

_____

** Describe what "He" has purposed in "Him"._____

_____

** What was His eternal goal?_____

_____

DQ: ** What does He have in mind for us in the fullness of the times?_____

_____

** When do you think that will be?_____

_____

Ephesians 1:10d-12 *In Him* **11** *also we have obtained an inheritance, having been predestined according to His purpose who works all things after the counsel of His will,* **12** *to the end that we who were the first to hope in Christ would be to the praise of His glory.*

FYI: See Glossary: *Predestination* for more information.

TQ: ** What else do we have "in Him"?_____

_____

** What did He predestine us for?_____

_____

DQ: ** What do you think our inheritance includes?_____

_____

Ephesians 1:13-14 *In Him, you also, after listening to the message of truth, the gospel of your salvation--having also* *believed, you were sealed in Him with the Holy Spirit of promise, **14** who is given as a pledge of our inheritance, with a view to the redemption of [God's own] possession, to the praise of His glory.*

TQ: ** What had we done to enable God to seal us with the Holy Spirit of promise?_____

_____

DQ: ** What does this sealing mean?_____

_____

** What is the pledge or guarantee of our future?_____

_____

** What possession of God will be redeemed?_____

_____

** "To the praise of His glory" is mentioned in Ephesians 1:6, 12, 14; what do you think it means?_____

_____

C-2   Paul's Prayer – Ephesians 1:15-19a

Ephesians 1:15-17   *For this reason I too, having heard of the faith in the Lord Jesus which [exists] among you and your love for all the saints, **16** do not cease giving thanks for you, while making mention [of you] in my prayers; **17** that the God of our Lord Jesus Christ, the Father of glory, may give to you a spirit of wisdom and of revelation in the knowledge of Him.*

TQ: ** What had Paul heard about the church?_____

_____

** What was his prayer?_____

_____

DQ: ** What would change if his prayer were answered?_____

_____

Ephesians 1:18-19a   *[I pray that] the eyes of your heart may be enlightened, so that you will know what is the hope of His calling, what are the riches of the glory of His inheritance in the saints, **19** and what is the surpassing greatness of His power toward us who believe.*

FYI: **Know** (Gk. *oida*) -- *to have seen or perceived, to know*

TQ: ** What else does he pray?_____

_____

     ** What is God's calling?_____

_____

     ** Explain what we should know._____

_____

DQ: ** Have you been called? _____ To what did He call you?_____

_____

     ** On a scale of one to ten, how well do you think you know these things?_____

     ** How will you be able to increase your level of knowledge and experience?_____

_____

C-3   The Father's Strength;
Christ's Exaltation -- Ephesians 1:19b-1:23

Ephesians 1:19b-21   *[These are] in accordance with the working of the strength of His might* **20** *which He brought about in Christ, when He raised Him from the dead and seated Him at His right hand in the heavenly [places],* **21** *far above all rule and authority and power and dominion, and every name that is named, not only in this age but also in the one to come.*

TQ: ** What does this passage tell us about the Father and the Son?

_____

_____

     ** Where was Christ?_____

_____

     ** Where is He now?_____

_____

DQ: ** Who has the might in verse 19?_____
     ** What is in accord with His might?_____

_____

Ephesians 1:22-23   *And He put all things in subjection under His feet, and gave Him as head over all things to the church,*

23 *which is His body, the fullness of Him who fills all in all.*

TQ: ** What does this passage tell us about the Father and the Son?

_____

_____

** What does it tell us about the church?_____

_____

DQ: ** What does this information about the church mean?_____

_____

C-4 God's Work on Our Behalf -- Ephesians 2:1-23

Ephesians 2:1-3   *And you were dead in your trespasses and sins,* **2** *in which you formerly walked according to the course of this world, according to the prince of the power of the air, of the spirit that is now working in the sons of disobedience.* **3** *Among them we too all formerly lived in the lusts of our flesh, indulging the desires of the flesh and of the mind, and were by nature children of wrath, even as the rest.*

TQ: ** List Paul's descriptions of their lives before believers came to Christ.

_____

_____

DQ: ** Who is the "prince of the power of the air"?_____

_____

** Who are the "sons of disobedience"?_____

_____

** What do you think it means to be "children of wrath"?_____

_____

Ephesians 2:4-7   *But God, being rich in mercy, because of His great love with which He loved us,* **5** *even when we were dead in our transgressions, made us alive together with Christ (by grace you have been saved),* **6** *and raised us up with Him, and seated us with Him in the heavenly [places] in Christ Jesus,* **7** *so that in the ages to come He might show the surpassing riches of His grace in kindness to-ward us in Christ Jesus.*

TQ: ** What does this passage tell us about God the Father?

_____

_____

** Trace the believer's journey from beginning to end._____

_____

** What does the future hold for those who believe in Christ?

_____

_____

** Why did He do this for us?_____

_____

** Where must we be to experience the fullness of God's kindness?

_____

_____

DQ: ** Explain salvation by grace from verse five._____

_____

** Where are you on the journey Paul described?_____

_____

Ephesians 2:8-10   _For by grace you have been saved through faith; and that not of yourselves, [it is] the gift of God;_ **9** _not as a result of works, so that no one may boast._ **10** _For we are His workmanship, created in Christ Jesus for good works, which God prepared beforehand so that we would walk in them._

TQ: ** Paul expanded on his brief statement in verse five. What did he clarify?_____

_____

** How and why are believers saved?_____

_____

** What did Paul say concerning works and salvation?_____

_____

DQ: ** Are you fulfilling what God intended for a believer?_____
** What good works are you involved in today?_____

_____

Ephesians 2:11-12   _Therefore remember that formerly you, the Gentiles in the flesh, who are called "Uncircumcision" by the so-called "Circumcision," [which is] performed in the flesh by human hands—_ **12** _[remember] that you were at that time separate from Christ, excluded from the com-_

monwealth of Israel, and strangers to the covenants of promise, having no hope and without God in the world.

FYI: Prior to Christ's death and resurrection, Gentiles had to become Jews to be included in God's Covenant. Christ's sacrifice changed that. Now both Jews and Gentiles must believe in Christ for the redemption of their sins and to be reconciled with God.

TQ: ** What are Gentiles called to remember?_____

Ephesians 2:13-16 *But now in Christ Jesus you who formerly were far off have been brought near by the blood of Christ.* **14** *For He Himself is our peace, who made both [groups into] one and broke down the barrier of the dividing wall,* **15** *by abolishing in His flesh the enmity, [which is] the Law of commandments [contained] in ordinances, so that in Himself He might make the two into one new man, [thus] establishing peace,* **16** *and might reconcile them both in one body to God through the cross, by it having put to death the enmity.*

FYI: **Enmity** (*echthra*) – *deep seated hatred, often mutual.*

DQ: ** Who are the two groups he is discussing?_____

** What happened to them?_____

** What was abolished and how did it happen?_____

** Explain in your own words what Paul is teaching in this passage.
_____
_____

Ephesians 2:17-22 *AND HE CAME AND PREACHED PEACE TO YOU WHO WERE FAR AWAY, AND PEACE TO THOSE WHO WERE NEAR;* **18** *for through Him we both have our access in one Spirit to the Father.* **19** *So then you are no longer strangers and aliens, but you are fellow citizens with the saints, and are of God's household,* **20** *having been built on the foundation of the apostles and prophets, Christ Jesus Himself being the corner [stone],* **21** *in whom* *the whole building, being fitted together, is growing into a holy temple in the Lord,* **22** *in whom you also are being built together into a dwelling of God in the Spirit.*

FYI: Verse 17 quotes from Isaiah 57:19.

TQ: ** Who are those who are far?_____

_____

          ** Who are those who are near?_____

_____

          ** What are they far or near from?_____

_____

          ** How did He establish peace?_____

_____

          ** What is the current standing of Gentile believers?_____

_____

          ** How does he describe the foundation and the temple for God's dwelling?_____

_____

          ** Where must we be for this to be true of us?_____

_____

B-2   The Mystery of Christ – Ephesians 3:1-21

C-1   The Mystery Explained -- Ephesians 3:1-13

Ephesians 3:1-3   *For this reason I, Paul, the prisoner of Christ Jesus for the sake of you Gentiles—***2** *if indeed you have heard of the stewardship of God's grace which was given to me for you;* **3** *that by revelation there was made known to me the mystery, as I wrote before in brief.*

TQ: ** For what reason?_____

_____

          ** What did Paul say about himself?_____

_____

Ephesians 3:4-7   *By referring to this, when you read you can understand my insight into the mystery of Christ,* **5** *which in other generations was not made known to the sons of men, as it has now been revealed to His holy apostles and prophets in the Spirit;* **6** *[to be specific], that the Gentiles* *are fellow heirs and fellow members of the body, and fellow partakers of the promise in Christ Jesus through the gospel, 7 of which I was made a minister, according to the gift of God's grace which was given to me according to the working of His power.*

FYI: A mystery in the New Testament is a truth that has been concealed in the past but has now been revealed. Several concepts in the New Testament are referred to as mysteries:

- The hardening of Israel so the Gentiles could come into the Kingdom (Romans 11:26, Colossians 1:26-27);
- The inclusion of both the Gentiles and the Jews into one body (Ephesians 3:3-6);
- The gospel, or salvation through faith in Christ (Romans 16:25, 1 Corinthians 2:7-8, Ephesians 6:19);
- The rapture of the living saints (1 Corinthians 15:51-52); and
- The church (Ephesians 5:32).

TQ: ** How does Paul define a mystery?_____

_____

** What mystery did he refer to?_____

_____

DQ: ** What works of God's grace has Paul mentioned so far in this letter?

_____

_____

Ephesians 3:8-10 *To me, the very least of all saints, this grace was given, to preach to the Gentiles the unfathomable riches of Christ, 9 and to bring to light what is the administration of the mystery which for ages has been hidden in God who created all things; 10 so that the manifold wisdom of God might now be made known through the church to the rulers and the authorities in the heavenly [places].*

FYI: **Unfathomable** (Gk. *anexichniastos*) – that which cannot be searched out; beyond comprehension.

TQ: ** What did Paul intend to be accomplished with his preaching?_____

_____

** How, when, and to whom, will the wisdom of God be revealed?

_____

_____

Ephesians 3:11-13   *[This was] in accordance with the eternal purpose which He carried out in Christ Jesus our Lord, 12 in whom we have boldness and confident access through faith in Him. 13 Therefore I ask you not to lose heart at my tribulations on your behalf, for they are your glory.*

TQ: ** What impact does God's eternal purpose have on us in this life?

_____

_____

DQ: ** Explain what you know of God's eternal purpose for those in Christ.

_____

_____

C-2   Paul's Prayer for the Church -- Ephesians 3:14-19

Ephesians 3:14-19   *For this reason I bow my knees before the Father, 15 from whom every family in heaven and on earth derives its name, 16 that He would grant you, according to the riches of His glory, to be strengthened with power through His Spirit in the inner man, 17 so that Christ may dwell in your hearts through faith; [and] that you, being rooted and grounded in love, 18 may be able to comprehend with all the saints what is the breadth and length and height and depth, 19 and to know the love of Christ which surpasses knowledge, that you may be filled up to all the fullness of God.*

TQ: ** What is Paul praying for in this passage?_____

_____

** What will change when this prayer is answered?_____

_____

C-3 Concluding Eulogy of Praise – Ephesians 3:20-21

Ephesians 3:20-21   *Now to Him who is able to do far more abundantly beyond all that we ask or think, according to the
power that works within us,* **21** *to Him [be] the glory in
the church and in Christ Jesus to all generations forever
and ever. Amen.*

TQ: ** Who is "Him" in this passage?_____

_____

** What is to go "to Him"?_____

_____

** How does it happen?_____

_____

A-3 WALK: Walking Worthy of Our Calling -- Ephesians 4:1-6:9

B-1 Walking in Unity – Ephesians 4:1-16

C-1 Attitudes to Preserve Unity – Ephesians 4:1-6

Ephesians 4:1-6   *Therefore I, the prisoner of the Lord, implore
you to walk in a manner worthy of the calling with which
you have been called,* **2** *with all humility and gentleness,
with patience, showing tolerance for one another in love,*
3 *being diligent to preserve the unity of the Spirit in the
bond of peace.* **4** *[There is] one body and one Spirit, just
as also you were called in one hope of your calling;* **5** *one
Lord, one faith, one baptism,* **6** *one God and Father of all
who is over all and through all and in all.*

TQ: ** What manner of walk is worthy of our calling?_____

_____

** Since we have been called and saved by grace, how should we live
with each other? (See Ephesians 2:8.)_____

_____

DQ: ** How should the grace of God characterize the way we treat others?

_____

_____

** With all the unity and oneness in our faith, where do the differences and divisions come from?_____

C-2   Gifts to Preserve Unity – Ephesians 4:7-13

Ephesians 4:7-9   *But to each one of us grace was given according to the measure of Christ's gift. 8 Therefore it says, "WHEN HE ASCENDED ON HIGH, HE LED CAPTIVE A HOST OF CAPTIVES, AND HE GAVE GIFTS TO MEN." 9 (Now this [expression], "He ascended," what does it mean except that He also had descended into the lower parts of the earth? 10 He who descended is Himself also He who ascended far above all the heavens, so that He might fill all things.)*

FYI: Verse 8 quotes from Psalm 68:18.

This passage describes Jesus' descent into Hades in order to relocate the spirits of dead believers into Paradise. (See the Glossary: *Eternal destinies* for an explanation of terms regarding life after death.)

Both Heaven and Hell are located in the spiritual realm and are not found in our physical universe. We refer to Heaven as being up, and Hell as being down or in "the lower parts of the earth" as a matter of convenience and convention. The heat and lava from a volcano (coming from the "lower parts of the earth") provide a vivid and dramatic analogy for the conditions of Hell and the Lake of Fire.

TQ: ** What two activities does this passage tell us that Christ accomplished on His ascent into heaven?_____

Ephesians 4:11-13   *And He gave some [as] apostles, and some [as] prophets, and some [as] evangelists, and some [as] pastors and teachers, 12 for the equipping of the saints for the work of service, to the building up of the body of Christ; 13 until we all attain to the unity of the faith, and of the knowledge of the Son of God, to a mature man, to the measure of the stature which belongs to the fullness of Christ.*

FYI: What Paul named is sometimes referred to as the 5-fold ministries. Each one is characterized by a different interest and concern as well as the ability that would correspond with that interest.

- **Apostle:** concerned with churches, pastors and leaders
- **Prophet:** concerned with holiness and man's relationship with God
- **Evangelist:** concerned with men's souls and their salvation
- **Pastor:** concerned with people, their growth and relationships
- **Teacher:** concerned with truth and its presentation.

TQ: ** What are the purposes of these ministries?_____

_____

** How long will they be practiced?_____

_____

DQ: ** Which one of these five ministries best reflects your concerns and interests?_____

_____

C-3   Love to Preserve Unity – Ephesians 4:14-16

Ephesians 4:14-16   *As a result, we are no longer to be children, tossed here and there by waves and carried about by every wind of doctrine, by the trickery of men, by craftiness in deceitful scheming;* **15** *but speaking the truth in love, we are to grow up in all [aspects] into Him who is the head, [even] Christ,* **16** *from whom the whole body, being fitted and held together by what every joint supplies, according to the proper working of each individual part, causes the growth of the body for the building up of itself in love.*

TQ: ** What characterizes the behavior of children?_____

_____

** What is the goal of our maturity?_____

_____

** How is that growth achieved?_____

_____

DQ: ** How well do you think you are doing in these instructions?

_____

_____

** What possible problems to unity are suggested in this passage?
_____
_____

B-2   Instructions for Walking in Christ – Ephesians 4:17-6:9

C-1   Put on Your New Self – Ephesians 4:17-5:21

Ephesians 4:17-19   *So this I say, and affirm together with the Lord, that you walk no longer just as the Gentiles also walk, in the futility of their mind, **18** being darkened in their understanding, excluded from the life of God because of the ignorance that is in them, because of the hardness of their heart; **19** and they, having become callous, have given themselves over to sensuality for the practice of every kind of impurity with greediness.*

TQ: ** Restate in your own words the spiritual lives of those without God.
_____

** Without God, what kinds of experiences do men (and women) pursue?_____
_____

DQ: ** Since you came to Christ, have you truly left that life or is some of it still hanging on?_____
_____

Ephesians 4:20-24   *But you did not learn Christ in this way, **21** if indeed you have heard Him and have been taught in Him, just as truth is in Jesus, **22** that, in reference to your former manner of life, you lay aside the old self, which is being corrupted in accordance with the lusts of deceit, **23** and that you be renewed in the spirit of your mind, **24** and put on the new self, which in [the likeness of] God has been created in righteousness and holiness of the truth.*

FYI: Old/New **Self** (Gk. *anthropos*) -- man, human. The King James Bible translated verse 22 as "laying aside the *old man*." It refers to the patterns of behavior that we had as non-believers.

TQ: ** Explain Paul's message concerning the old and new selves.

_____

_____

** What direction is "the old self" heading?_____

** What are we to do with "the old self"?_____

** What are we to do with the "new self"?_____

_____

DQ: ** What does it mean to "learn Christ"?_____

** What have you learned of Christ?_____

** How did you learn it?_____

** What does this passage suggest is the key ingredient to changing your behavior? (See Romans 12:2.)_____

_____

Ephesians 4:25-27   _Therefore, laying aside falsehood, SPEAK TRUTH EACH ONE [of you] WITH HIS NEIGHBOR, for we are members of one another. **26** BE ANGRY, AND [yet] DO NOT SIN; do not let the sun go down on your anger, **27** and do not give the devil an opportunity._

FYI: Verse 25 quotes from Zechariah 8:16.
Verse 26 quotes from Psalm 4:4.

TQ: ** Instead of lying, as "the old self" would have done, what are we to do?_____

_____

DQ: ** Instead of sinning in our anger, what are we to do?_____

** What opportunity would we be giving to the devil?_____

_____

Ephesians 4:28   _He who steals must steal no longer; but rather he must labor, performing with his own hands what is good, so that he will have [something] to share with one who has need._

TQ: ** Instead of stealing, what should "the new self" be doing?

_____

_____

Ephesians 4:29   *Let no unwholesome word proceed from your mouth, but only such [a word] as is good for edification according to the need [of the moment], so that it will give grace to those who hear.*

FYI: Are you seeing the contrast between the behavior of the old self and that of the new self that Christ is developing in each of us?
Ephesians 4:29 is a good verse to memorize.

TQ: ** What patterns of speech should we be using?_____

_____

DQ: ** What are unwholesome words?_____

_____

Ephesians 4:30-32   *Do not grieve the Holy Spirit of God, by whom you were sealed for the day of redemption.* **31** *Let all bitterness and wrath and anger and clamor and slander be put away from you, along with all malice.* **32** *Be kind to one another, tender-hearted, forgiving each other, just as God in Christ also has forgiven you.*

FYI: **Sealed** (Gk. *sphragizo*) – providing the sign of identification or ownership. The presence of the Holy Spirit in the lives of believers will serve to identify them as belonging to Christ at His return.

TQ: ** What behaviors grieve the Holy Spirit?_____

_____

** What please Him?_____

_____

Ephesians 5:1-2   *Therefore be imitators of God, as beloved children;* **2** *and walk in love, just as Christ also loved you and gave Himself up for us, an offering and a sacrifice to God as a fragrant aroma.*

TQ: ** How did Christ walk?_____

_____

DQ: ** Describe examples of how little children imitate their parents in speech and behavior._____

** Do you see yourself doing the same kind of imitating?_____
** Who or what are you imitating?_____

** Is it easier to imitate good behavior or bad?_____
** Why is that?_____

_____

Ephesians 5:3-5　　*But immorality or any impurity or greed must not even be named among you, as is proper among saints; **4** and [there must be no] filthiness and silly talk, or coarse jesting, which are not fitting, but rather giving of thanks. **5** For this you know with certainty, that no immoral or impure person or covetous man, who is an idolater, has an inheritance in the kingdom of Christ and God.*

FYI:　　**Immorality / immoral person**: (Gk. *porneia / pornos*) – any kind of extramarital, unlawful, or unnatural sexual intercourse; *prostitution, fornication, adultery.*
　　Impurity / impure person: (Gk. *akatharsia / akathartos*) – *unclean, impure, defilement, moral decay and rottenness, indecency, sexual impurity.*
** **Greed / covetous man**: (Gk. *pleonexia / pleonektes*) –, a disposition to have more than one's share; *avarice, covetousness, a greedy or grasping person.*

TQ: ** What behaviors must we avoid as Christians?_____

_____

** Why are we to avoid them?_____

_____

** What is one speech pattern we are urged to adopt in this passage?

_____

_____

Ephesians 5:6-9　　*Let no one deceive you with empty words, for because of these things the wrath of God comes upon the sons of disobedience. **7** Therefore do not be partakers with them; **8** for you were formerly darkness, but now you are Light in the Lord; walk as children of Light **9** (for the fruit of the Light [consists] in all goodness and right-*

eousness and truth), **10** *trying to learn what is pleasing to the Lord.*

TQ: ** What behavior causes the wrath of God to eventually fall?

_____

** What characterizes the result of walking in the light?

_____
_____

DQ: ** Explain the difference between walking in darkness and walking in light._____

_____
** Does verse 10 describe you?_____
** Why do you suppose finding the will of God is sometimes difficult?

_____
_____

Ephesians 5:11-12 *Do not participate in the unfruitful deeds of darkness, but instead even expose them;* **12** *for it is disgraceful even to speak of the things which are done by them in secret.*

FYI: In Galatians 5, Paul listed the *deeds* of the flesh and the *fruit* of the Spirit.

DQ: ** Why did he consider the deeds of darkness (or the flesh) to be unfruitful?_____

_____
** Why does darkness produce *deeds* and light produce *fruit*?

_____
_____
** How do you expose behavior without speaking about it?

_____
_____
** What does Paul say we should do?_____

_____

Ephesians 5:13-14 *But all things become visible when they are exposed by the light, for everything that becomes visible is light.* **14** *for this reason it says, "Awake, sleeper, And arise from the dead, And Christ will shine on you."*

FYI: Verse 14 is not a quote from the Old Testament. "It says" is a verb in the third person and could also be translated "he (or she, or it) says". Paul is probably telling us God's direction in what we should be doing ("He says"). It is also possible that he is quoting from something like a hymn or a chorus the church was singing at that time.

DQ: ** Explain what Paul means in this passage?_____

_____

** What behavior should we be "putting on" according to this verse?

_____

_____

Ephesians 5:15-17   *Therefore be careful how you walk, not as unwise men but as wise,* **16** *making the most of your time, because the days are evil.* **17** *So then do not be foolish, but understand what the will of the Lord is.*

DQ: ** How do we make the most of our time?_____

_____

** What do wise people understand?_____

_____

** How do wise people walk?_____

_____

** What does a foolish person not understand?_____

_____

** What does verse 17 suggest in light of verse 10?_____

_____

Ephesians 5:18-21   *And do not get drunk with wine, for that is dissipation, but be filled with the Spirit,* **19** *speaking to one another in psalms and hymns and spiritual songs, singing and making melody with your heart to the Lord;* **20** *always giving thanks for all things in the name of our Lord Jesus Christ to God, even the Father;* **21** *and be subject to one another in the fear of Christ.*

FYI: **Dissipation** (Gk. *asotia*) -- the act of one who has abandoned himself to reckless, immoral behavior; *debauchery, incorrigibility.*

     If we were to change the punctuation of this passage, it would make better sense to us. It should read: "*...be filled with the Spirit as you are speaking to one another. In psalms and hymns and spiritual songs, be* *singing and making melody with your heart to the Lord...*" There is no punctuation in the original texts.

DQ: ** How would you characterize an individual who was filled with the Spirit?_____

_____

** How can we be subject to one another? _____

_____

** Why should we be?_____

_____

C-2 RE: Specific Relationships – Ephesians 5:22-6:9

D-1 Husbands and Wives – Ephesians 5:22-33

Ephesians 5:22-24   *Wives, [be subject] to your own husbands, as to the Lord. 23 For the husband is the head of the wife, as Christ also is the head of the church, He Himself [being] the Savior of the body. 24 But as the church is subject to Christ, so also the wives [ought to be] to their husbands in everything.*

FYI: Even though this passage addresses wives, the behavior being discussed is clearly the husband's. A wife responds to the actions that are initiated by her husband. Any wife who has a husband who is her savior (willing to lay down his life for her) would gladly submit, or be subject, to him.

The following describes how Christ became the savior of his bride, the church, and how the husband can become the savior of his wife. It is an accurate description of love commanded in verse 25.

-- 1. He makes what seems to be HER problem, HIS problem.

-- 2. He applies all his resources and abilities to resolve what is now HIS problem.

-- 3. He lays down his life, even to the point of death, to resolve HIS problem.

TQ: ** Why should the wife be subject to her husband?_____

_____

DQ: ** Look back to verse 21. Does the husband ever submit to his wife?

_____

** Reconcile verses 21 and 22?_____

_____

** Describe what you have observed concerning the Church being sub-ject to Christ._____

** What would be different if we were totally subject to Christ?
_____

** Do you suppose that "unsubmissive" wives are simply imitating the pattern of (non-)submissiveness that their husbands demonstrate for them?_____
** Explain your thinking._____
_____

Ephesians 5:25-27   *Husbands, love your wives, just as Christ also loved the church and gave Himself up for her, 26 so that He might sanctify her, having cleansed her by the wash-ing of water with the word, 27 that He might present to Himself the church in all her glory, having no spot or wrinkle or any such thing; but that she would be holy and blameless.*

TQ: ** How did Christ love the church?_____
_____

** What specific action did He take?_____

** What goal did He have in mind?_____
_____

DQ: ** How can a husband give himself up for his wife?_____
_____

** How can he wash her with his words?_____
_____

** What is the glory of the church?_____
_____

** What do you suppose is the glory of the wife?_____
_____

** What would be the glory of the husband?_____
_____

Ephesians 5:28-30   *So husbands ought also to love their own wives as their own bodies. He who loves his own wife loves himself; 29 for no one ever hated his own flesh, but nourishes and cherishes it, just as Christ also [does] the church, 30 because we are members of His body.*

FYI: **Nourishes**: (Gk. *ektrepho*) – to bring to maturity; *educate, to feed or nourish.*
Cherishes: (Gk. *thalpo*) -- *to warm, comfort, tenderly care for.*

TQ: ** How should a husband love his wife?_____
_____

DQ: ** Once again, in this passage, Christ becomes the pattern for us to follow. Do you (and your spouse) see the life of Christ being lived out in
your relationship? _____ Explain._____
_____

Ephesians 5:31-32   *FOR THIS REASON A MAN SHALL LEAVE HIS
FATHER AND MOTHER AND SHALL BE JOINED TO HIS
WIFE, AND THE TWO SHALL BECOME ONE FLESH.
32 This mystery is great; but I am speaking with reference to Christ and the church.*

FYI: Verse 31 quotes from Genesis 2:24.
The process of developing oneness between a husband and wife is
not an easy one and does not happen in a single day. Most marriages
that end in divorce fail because both the husband and wife insist on
maintaining their independence. A husband and wife will experience
true marital happiness when they develop a oneness in the three areas
of body, soul and spirit.

TQ: ** Who leaves mother and father?_____

DQ: ** What does the wife do?_____
_____

** How does this work?_____
_____

** How does the relationship between Christ and the church provide a
model for the relationship between the husband and wife?
_____
_____

Ephesians 5:33   *Nevertheless, each individual among you also
is to love his own wife even as himself, and the wife must
[see to it] that she respects her husband.*

TQ: ** From this passage, what does the husband need from the wife?
_____
_____

** What does the wife need from the relationship?_____

** What do these things look like when they are put into practice?

_____

D-2 Children and Fathers – Ephesians 6:1-4

Ephesians 6:1-3   *Children, obey your parents in the Lord, for this is right.* **2** *HONOR YOUR FATHER AND MOTHER (which is the first commandment with a promise),* **3** *SO THAT IT MAY BE WELL WITH YOU, AND THAT YOU MAY LIVE LONG ON THE EARTH.*

FYI: Verses 2 and 3 quote from Exodus 20:12 and Deuteronomy 5:16.

The way a child obeys his parents is how he will obey his Heavenly Father. If the child does not learn to obey his parents when he is young, it will be very difficult for him to obey God when he is older.

The Ten Commandments were first given and recorded in Exodus 20 by Moses at the beginning of the wilderness wanderings. They were repeated years later just before Moses' death and recorded again in Deuteronomy 5.

There are probably many reasons for living a long life, but one is contained in the idea that this life is the gestation period to prepare us for eternity. We have only 70-80 years (Psalm 90:10) to learn how to live like Christ and to rule with Him (Revelation 20:6). We need all the time we can get.

Thinking of this life as a gestation period for eternity solves a number of dilemnas for us. A baby in the womb has no need for arms or legs, but they are being devloped for the next stage of his life. We often question why we are going through some difficulty, but God is developing "arms and legs" that we don't need now, but which will equip us for our eternal purposes. Could this be why Paul tells us to give thanks for "all things" (Ephesians 5:20)?

The blessing of a long life is proof that the purpose of our salvation is not to get us to heaven. If that were the goal, God would take us as soon as we believe in Christ. No, He is preparing His people for greater things than just Heaven.

TQ: ** What is the benefit for the child to honor his or her parents?

_____

_____

DQ: ** Review Exodus 20; do any other commandments have a promise associated with them?_____

** How can children honor their fathers and mothers?_____

** What advantage do you see for living a long life?_____

Ephesians 6:4 *Fathers, do not provoke your children to anger, but bring them up in the discipline and instruction of the Lord.*

DQ: ** In your experience, how do fathers tend to provoke their children?

** Name practical ways fathers can bring up their children in the discipline and instruction of the Lord?_____

D-3 Employers and Employees – Ephesians 6:5-9

Ephesians 6:5-8 *Slaves, be obedient to those who are your masters according to the flesh, with fear and trembling, in the sincerity of your heart, as to Christ; 6 not by way of eyeservice, as men-pleasers, but as slaves of Christ, doing the will of God from the heart. 7 With good will render service, as to the Lord, and not to men, 8 knowing that whatever good thing each one does, this he will receive back from the Lord, whether slave or free.*

FYI: In our modern culture, our economy is no longer based on slavery. These verses, however, apply equally well to those in an employee and employer relationship.

TQ: ** How should employees behave in the workplace?_____

** Why should they do this?_____

DQ: ** Does your work ethic demonstrate that you are working for the Lord in your employment?_____

Ephesians 6:9   *And masters, do the same things to them, and give up threatening, knowing that both their Master and yours is in heaven, and there is no partiality with Him.*

TQ: ** What is "the same thing" that masters are to do?_____

_____

** What does this passage tell us about God?_____

_____

** How would an employer correct an employee according to this verse?_____

_____

A-4 STAND: Standing Firm in Christ – Ephesians 6:10-20

B-1 Put on the Armor of God – Ephesians 6:10-17

Ephesians 6:10-12   *Finally, be strong in the Lord and in the strength of His might.* **11** *Put on the full armor of God, so that you will be able to stand firm against the schemes of the devil.* **12** *For our struggle is not against flesh and blood, but against the rulers, against the powers, against the world forces of this darkness, against the spiritual [forces] of wickedness in the heavenly [places].*

FYI: Verse 12 suggests that there is a hierarchy with varying degrees of authority and responsibility among the demonic (fallen angel) kingdom. Daniel 10:12-13, 20-21 describe a battle between "princes" in the spiritual realm.

- **Rulers** (Gk. *arche*) – *beginning, origin, the first.*
- **Powers** (Gk. *exousia*) – *power to act, authority, dominion.*
- **World forces of the darkness** (Gk. *kosmokrator* and *skotos*) -- *Kosmokrtator is a ruler of this world,* one holding power over parts of the world. *Skotos* refers to *darkness* as an absence of moral and spiritual light and life, evil.
- **Spiritual [forces] of wickedness** (Gk. *pneumatikos* and *poneria*) -- the practice of *evil, wickedness and malice* in the spiritual realm.

TQ: ** Why should we put on the armor of God?_____

_____

** Who is our fight with?_____

** Who are the ones we do not fight?_____

Ephesians 6:13-17   *Therefore, take up the full armor of God, so that you will be able to resist in the evil day, and having done everything, to stand firm.* **14** *Stand firm therefore, HAVING GIRDED YOUR LOINS WITH TRUTH, and HAVING PUT ON THE BREASTPLATE OF RIGHTEOUSNESS,* **15** *and having shod YOUR FEET WITH THE PREPARATION OF THE GOSPEL OF PEACE;* **16** *in addition to all, taking up the shield of faith with which you will be able to extinguish all the flaming arrows of the evil [one].* **17** *And take THE HELMET OF SALVATION, and the sword of the Spirit, which is the word of God.*

FYI: Verse 14 quotes from Isaiah 59:17.
Verse 15 quotes from Isaiah 52:7.
Verse 17 quotes from Isaiah 59:17.
Isaiah has some of the same imagery from the warfare of his day, but Paul identified the spiritual significance of the armor of a Roman soldier.

Word (Gk. *rhema*) – the word that God speaks in our hearts or spirits. (See Glossary: *Word*.)

TQ: ** What does the armor of God enable us to do?

DQ: ** What is the spiritual significance of each item of armor?

_____

** What are we to do when we have clothed ourselves with armor?

_____

** What does this mean?_____

** What items are for our defense or protection?_____

** Which items are used for our offense or fighting?_____

** In your own words, what does this passage tell us to do?

_____

B-2 Pray at All Times– Ephesians 6:18-20

Ephesians 6:18-20 *With all prayer and petition pray at all times in the Spirit, and with this in view, be on the alert with all perseverance and petition for all the saints, **19** and [pray] on my behalf, that utterance may be given to me in the opening of my mouth, to make known with boldness the mystery of the gospel, **20** for which I am an ambassador in chains; that in [proclaiming] it I may speak boldly, as I ought to speak.*

FYI: *Praying in the Spirit* could be understood to mean: 1) praying according to the promptings of the Holy Spirit, or 2) praying in an unknown prayer language or tongue as in 1 Corinthians 14:2, 4, 15.

TQ: ** Having put the armor on, what are we to do?_____

_____

** What was Paul's personal prayer request?_____

_____

DQ: ** Think of the things you usually ask for when you pray. Was Paul concerned about these things?_____

_____

** What was His major interest?_____

_____

** What is ours?_____

_____

A-5 Conclusion – Ephesians 6:21-24

Ephesians 6:21-22 *But that you also may know about my circumstances, how I am doing, Tychicus, the beloved brother and faithful minister in the Lord, will make everything known to you. **22** I have sent him to you for this very purpose, so that you may know about us, and that he may comfort your hearts.*

TQ: ** How did Paul describe Tychicus?_____

_____

** What does he expect him to do?_____

_____

Ephesians 6:23-24 *Peace be to the brethren, and love with faith, from God the Father and the Lord Jesus Christ.* **24** *Grace be with all those who love our Lord Jesus Christ with incorruptible [love].*

TQ: ** What are the components of this blessing?_____

_____

DQ: ** How would this blessing change our lives if we received and lived its fullness?_____

_____

RECAP: List the characteristics of Christ that Paul mentions in this letter.

List the benefits that come to us because we are "in Christ."_____

How do we walk in a way that is pleasing to God? List specific behaviors and attitudes._____

Describe how to take a stand for Christ._____

Philippians: A Study Guide for LIFE

Outline and Table of Contents

Background Information

AUTHOR: Paul and Timothy, bond-servants of Jesus Christ (Philippians 1:1). It is universally understood that Paul was the actual writer of the letter and Timothy was merely his companion and co-worker in Rome.

DATE: The epistle or letter to the Philippians was most likely written about 62-63 AD, toward the end of Paul's house arrest in Rome (Acts 28).

THEME: This letter is a heartfelt message from a man who was unjustly in prison and awaiting trial because he appealed to Caesar to escape death by the Jews in Jerusalem. Read about his arrest and imprisonment in Acts 21-28.

        We might think that Paul would be motivated to get out of prison, but he has a different goal in mind. Rather than look at the urgency of his plans and the passing of time, he is guided by the compass of his mission; namely, knowing Christ, the power of His resurrection, the fellow-ship of His suffering, and ultimately, attaining the rewards of his own resurrection.

He also took the opportunity in this letter to explain the compass headings that guided Jesus' life and led to His final exaltation in Heaven. That compass provided the basis for the advice Paul gives the church in Philippi. He urges them to adopt the same attitudes that Christ had and reminds them, and us, to pursue the unity, attitudes and maturity that will benefit us most when Christ rewards us for our efforts on His behalf.

Philippians – A Study Guide for LIFE

A-1 Salutation – Philippians 1:1-2

Philippians 1:1-2   *Paul and Timothy, bond-servants of Christ Je-sus, To all the saints in Christ Jesus who are in Philippi, in-cluding the overseers and deacons:* **2** *Grace to you and peace from God our Father and the Lord Jesus Christ.*

TQ: ** Who wrote this letter?_____

_____

** To whom was it written?_____

_____

** What is the blessing?_____

_____

** To which group in the church does the letter seem to be primarily written?_____

_____

A-2 Paul's Affection for the Philippians – Philippians 1:3-11

Philippians 1:3-6   *I thank my God in all my remembrance of you,* **4** *always offering prayer with joy in my every prayer for you all,* **5** *in view of your participation in the gospel from the first day until now.* **6** *[For I am] confident of this very thing, that He who began a good work in you will perfect it until the day of Christ Jesus.*

FYI: Verse 6 would be good to memorize. No matter your situation, God is not finished with you yet, so take hope in *His* ability.

TQ: ** Describe Paul's pattern of prayer for the Philippian church._____

_____

** What did they do to make Paul feel the way he did?

_____

_____

DQ: ** How do you suppose they participated in the gospel?

_____

_____

Philippians 1:7-8   *For it is only right for me to feel this way about you all, because I have you in my heart, since both in my imprisonment and in the defense and confirmation of the gospel, you all are partakers of grace with me. **8** For God is my witness, how I long for you all with the affection of Christ Jesus.*

FYI: In Philippians 4:14-19, Paul explains their partnership with him.

TQ: ** How did Paul feel about the church in Philippi?_____

_____

** What was Paul's situation?_____

_____

DQ: ** How was the church a "partaker of grace" with Paul?_____

_____

Philippians 1:9-11   *And this I pray, that your love may abound still more and more in real knowledge and all discernment, **10** so that you may approve the things that are excellent, in order to be sincere and blameless until the day of Christ; **11** having been filled with the fruit of righteousness which [comes] through Jesus Christ, to the glory and praise of God.*

TQ: ** What was Paul's prayer for the church?_____

_____

** To what end was he praying these things?_____

_____

DQ: ** What change would their neighbors see when the prayer was answered?_____

_____

** In what context would they "approve the things that were excellent"?

_____

_____

A-3 Paul's Situation -- Philippians 1:12-2:4

B-1 Paul's Situation Described -- Philippians 1:12-26

Philippians 1:12-14   _Now I want you to know, brethren, that my circumstances have turned out for the greater progress of the gospel, **13** so that my imprisonment in [the cause of] Christ has become well known throughout the whole praetorian guard and to everyone else, **14** and that most of the brethren, trusting in the Lord because of my imprisonment, have far more courage to speak the word of God without fear._

FYI: In Rome, the **Praetorium** was the living place for the guards of the emperor. In Jerusalem, the Praetorium was the governor's official residence (Matthew 27:27).

Paul had planned to continue his missionary journey, even going as far as Spain (Romans 15:24, 28). God had revealed that Paul was "to bear [Christ's] name before the Gentiles and kings and the sons of Israel" (Acts 9:15), yet he was now stuck in a Roman prison.

His future was uncertain, He was appealing to Caesar to resolve a Jewish compliant (Acts 21-28/), but his crime against Rome would have been worshipping and preaching the Lord Jesus (instead of Lord Caesar of Rome). Rome was tolerant of other religions, but any subversion or rebellion against Rome or the Emperor was a capital offense. His judgment could go either way; he could be killed or released.

Paul was a Roman citizen (Acts 22:27-28) so if the sentence were death, he would have been beheaded instead of crucified. Criminals who were citizens of Rome were killed in a more merciful manner than non-Romans.

The Bible does not record how Paul died, but tradition tells us that Paul was released from prison and continued to preach Jesus in unreached regions, including Spain. He was eventual re-arrested in Rome and beheaded during the reign of Nero.

TQ: ** What benefit did Paul see in his imprisonment?_____

_____

DQ: ** What negative circumstances in your life have ultimately exalted God?_____

_____

Philippians 1:15-16   *Some, to be sure, are preaching Christ even from envy and strife, but some also from good will;* **16** *the latter [do it] out of love, knowing that I am appointed for the defense of the gospel;* **17** *the former proclaim Christ out of selfish ambition rather than from pure motives, thinking to cause me distress in my imprisonment.*

TQ: ** Paul mentions two different motives for preaching the gospel. Identify and explain each one._____

_____

DQ: ** Identify other possible motives for preaching the gospel._____

** Can the wrong motive still exalt Christ?_____

_____

Philippians 1:18-21   *What then? Only that in every way, whether in pretense or in truth, Christ is proclaimed; and in this I rejoice. Yes, and I will rejoice,* **19** *for I know that this will turn out for my deliverance through your prayers and the provision of the Spirit of Jesus Christ,* **20** *according to my earnest expectation and hope, that I will not be put to shame in anything, but [that] with all boldness, Christ will even now, as always, be exalted in my body, whether by life or by death.* **21** *For to me, to live is Christ and to die is gain.*

FYI: **Deliverance** (Gk. *soteria*) -- *Salvation, deliverance, preservation, safety.*

TQ: ** How did Paul feel about those who preached from wrong motives?

_____

** Paul was uncertain of his future, but what was his great desire?

_____

_____

DQ: ** What did Paul mean by his "deliverance"?_____

_____

** This passage could be seen as Paul's compass heading or guiding light. How would you describe it?_____
_____

** What is your compass heading?_____
_____

Philippians 1:22-24   *But if [I am] to live [on] in the flesh, this [will mean] fruitful labor for me; and I do not know which to choose. 23 But I am hard-pressed from both [directions], having the desire to depart and be with Christ, for [that] is very much better; 24 yet to remain on in the flesh is more necessary for your sake.*

TQ: ** Paul explains that "deliverance" could be in two directions. How did he summarize each direction?_____
_____

** Which path does he seem to prefer?_____
_____

DQ: ** What is "fruitful labor" in the Christian's life?_____
_____

Philippians 1:25-26   *Convinced of this, I know that I will remain and continue with you all for your progress and joy in the faith, 26 so that your proud confidence in me may abound in Christ Jesus through my coming to you again.*

TQ: ** He expressed more confidence as he wrote. What path did Paul expect to happen at this point?_____
_____

** What did he tell us about the Philippian church and his expectations for it?_____
_____

B-2 Paul's Situation Applied – Philippians 1:27-2:4

Philippians 1:27-28   *Only conduct yourselves in a manner worthy of the gospel of Christ, so that whether I come and see you or remain absent, I will hear of you that you are standing firm in one spirit, with one mind striving together for the faith of the gospel; 28 in no way alarmed by [your] oppo-*

nents-- which is a sign of destruction for them, but of salvation for you, and that [too], from God.

TQ: ** What kind of conduct is worthy of the gospel of Christ?_____

** What unity did he want their reputation to reflect? (Add your insights from Philippians 2:1-2 to make a comprehensive list.)_____

** What attitude did he want them to have in the midst of persecution?
_____
_____

DQ: ** Paul demonstrated a lack of alarm in his situation; can you resolve to have the same response in all of life's situations?_____
_____

Philippians 1:29-30 *For to you it has been granted for Christ's sake, not only to believe in Him, but also to suffer for His sake,* **30** *experiencing the same conflict which you saw in me, and now hear [to be] in me.*

TQ: ** What can Christians expect to experience in their lives?_____
_____

DQ: ** What conflict was Paul experiencing?_____

** Persecution may come to us in these last days. What can we do to prepare for it?_____
_____

Philippians 2:1-2 *Therefore if there is any encouragement in Christ, if there is any consolation of love, if there is any fellowship of the Spirit, if any affection and compassion,* **2** *make my joy complete by being of the same mind, maintaining the same love, united in spirit, intent on one purpose.*

FYI: **Encouragement** (Gk. paraklesis) – *Calling to one's aid, encouragement, comfort, exhortation.*
Consolation (Gk. *paramuthion*) – A persuasive power that points to a basis for hope and provides incentive: *encouragement, comfort.*
Fellowship (Gk. *koinonia*) – A relationship characterized by sharing

everything in common: *fellowship, participation.*

Affection (Gk. *splagchnon*) – Literally, *intestines, inward parts of the body, the belly*; figuratively, the deep inner seat of tender emotions in the whole personality, variously thought of as the heart, stomach, bowels: *emotions, affection, tender.*

Compassion (Gk. *oiktirmos*) -- A tender emotion motivating one to help another: *sympathy, mercy, pity.*

Purpose (Gk. *phroneo*) – *Understanding, thoughts, intent, purpose.*

The "if" statements in this paragraph are not in doubt in Paul's mind. He firmly believes these statements are true and expects the church to agree with them. The expected positive answer to each one is the strength of his statement and request.

TQ: ** What do these statements affirm in the life of the church?

_____

_____

** Do you agree that these statements are true?_____

** Explain your answer._____

_____

** What did he want them to do?_____

_____

** Add the points of unity from this passage to your list from Philippians 1:27-28. What are the key points of unity?_____

_____

DQ: ** Why does Paul mention these "if" conditions to their response to uni-ty?_____

_____

Philippians 2:3-4   *Do nothing from selfishness or empty conceit, but with humility of mind regard one another as more important than yourselves; 4 do not [merely] look out for your own personal interests, but also for the interests of others.*

TQ: ** There are two directions of life presented in this passage. Describe each path._____

_____

** What does Paul want the church to do?_____

_____

DQ: ** How well is your church doing this?_____

_____

** How well are you doing it?_____

A-4 The Compass Christ Followed – Philippians 2:5-18

B-1 Christ's Compass Described– Philippians 2:5-11

Philippians 2:5-7   *Have this attitude in yourselves which was also in Christ Jesus, 6 who, although He existed in the form of God, did not regard equality with God a thing to be grasped, 7 but emptied Himself, taking the form of a bond-servant, [and] being made in the likeness of men.*

FYI: **Emptied** (Gk. *kenoo*) – *To empty, make empty; to make void, deprive of force, render vain, useless.*
This passage is referred to as the *kenosis* of Christ -- His self-emptying. He laid aside the use of His divine attributes (emptying Himself) to assume the form and role of a bond-servant (Hebrews 2:14, 17; 4:15).

TQ: ** What is the key point in this passage so far?_____

DQ: ** How would someone live out this attitude?_____

Philippians 2:8-11   *Being found in appearance as a man, He humbled Himself by becoming obedient to the point of death, even death on a cross. 9 For this reason also, God highly exalted Him, and bestowed on Him the name which is above every name, 10 so that at the name of Jesus EVERY KNEE WILL BOW, of those who are in heaven and on earth and under the earth, 11 and that every tongue will confess that Jesus Christ is Lord, to the glory of God the Father.*

FYI: Verse 10 quotes from Isaiah 45:23.
Jesus traveled the greatest distance possible in His humiliation. He went from the highest heaven to lowest man: not to nobility, not middle class, not even the lower class, but to servanthood (Mark 10:45). As a servant, He humbled Himself even lower, to be considered and crucified as a criminal. It is for this reason that He is highly exalted; His exal-

tation is an *earned* position.

Every knee will bow and every person will eventually acknowledge the Lordship of Christ. If they bow in this life they will be saved, forgiven of their sin and welcomed into God's family. Many people, however, will persist in their rebellious independence (Matthew 7:13-14), so their bowing in submission will take place at the Great White Throne Judgment (Revelation 20:11-15). Christ will pass judgment on them and send them to an eternity in the Lake of Fire, but there will be no opportunity for them to roll the clock back and do their lives over. (See Glossary: *Eternal destinies.*)

DQ: ** How could we reproduce this attitude of emptying in our own lives?

_____

** What effect will emptying ourselves have on our ability to do God's will?_____

_____

B-2 Christ's Compass Applied – Philippians 2:12-18

Philippians 2:12-13 *So then, my beloved, just as you have always obeyed, not as in my presence only, but now much more in my absence, work out your salvation with fear and trembling;* **13** *for it is God who is at work in you, both to will and to work for [His] good pleasure.*

FYI: In our salvation, God has implanted desires, attitudes and giftings in us that we need to work out in practical living. The last part of verse 12 and all of verse 13 are good verses to memorize.

TQ: ** When we "work out" our salvation, Who is also working?_____
** Explain._____

_____

DQ: ** What kinds of things should we be "working out"?_____

_____

Philippians 2:14-16 *Do all things without grumbling or disputing;* **15** *so that you will prove yourselves to be blameless and innocent, children of God above reproach in the midst of a crooked and perverse generation, among whom you appear as lights in the world,* **16** *holding fast the word of* *life, so that in the day of Christ I will have reason to glory because I did not run in vain nor toil in vain.*

FYI: **Grumble** (Gk. *goggusmos*) – An expression of dissatisfaction: *grumbling, complaining, muttering, murmuring, whispering, secret talk.*
Disputing (Gk. *dialogismos*) – *Doubt, dispute, argument.*
Word of Life (Gk. *logos* of *zoe*) -- The divine revelation of God's life.

TQ: ** What does he tell us to do?_____

** What will it prove?_____

** What did Paul call the church in this passage?_____

** Explain what we are to hold fast._____

** Explain why we are to do so._____

Philippians 2:17-18   *But even if I am being poured out as a drink offering upon the sacrifice and service of your faith, I rejoice and share my joy with you all.* **18** *You too, [I urge you], rejoice in the same way and share your joy with me.*

FYI: A **drink offering** was an offering of a liquid (usually wine) that was poured out on the ground or on a sacrifice as an expression of worship to God. One of the best illustrations of a drink offering is David pouring out the water of Bethlehem that his soldiers risked their lives to get for him (2 Samuel 23:15-27). Paul is using this imagery to convey that even if his life is a complete waste in human terms, it is poured out in worship to God upon a sacrifice that the church in Philippi had made.

TQ: ** Explain in your own words how Paul's life was a drink offering.

_____

_____

DQ: ** What joy do you suppose Paul found in his situation?_____

** What sacrifice do you think the Philippian church had made?

_____

_____

A-5 Helpers for Philippi – Philippians 2:19-30

   B-1 Timothy – Philippians 2:19-24

Philippians 2:19-21   *But I hope in the Lord Jesus to send Timothy to you shortly, so that I also may be encouraged when I learn of your condition.* **20** *For I have no one [else] of kindred spirit who will genuinely be concerned for your welfare.* **21** *For they all seek after their own interests, not those of Christ Jesus.*

TQ: ** What was Timothy supposed to do?_____
_____
** What did Paul tell us about Timothy and the other people who were with him?_____
_____

DQ: ** Did Paul's reaction to the attitude of those who seek their own interests flavor the advice he gives the church in Philippi?_____
_____
** What advice was applicable?_____
_____

Philippians 2:22-24   *But you know of his proven worth, that he served with me in the furtherance of the gospel like a child [serving] his father.* **23** *Therefore I hope to send him immediately, as soon as I see how things [go] with me;* **24** *and I trust in the Lord that I myself also will be coming shortly.*

TQ: ** What else did he tell us about Timothy?_____
_____
** What were Paul's plans for himself and Timothy?_____
_____

   B-2 Epaphroditus – Philippians 2:25-30

Philippians 2:25-27   *But I thought it necessary to send to you Epaphroditus, my brother and fellow worker and fellow soldier, who is also your messenger and minister to my need;* **26** *because he was longing for you all and was distressed* *because you had heard that he was sick. **27** For indeed he was sick to the point of death, but God had mercy on him, and not on him only but also on me, so that I would not have sorrow upon sorrow.*

FYI: **Epaphroditus** (*"lovely"*). His name comes from the name of *Aphrodite*, a Greek goddess. In Roman mythology, *Aphrodite* was called *Venus*.

TQ: ** What did Paul tell us about Epaphroditus?_____

_____

DQ: ** Paul had done many miracles in his ministry (Acts 19:11-12), but Epaphroditus was sick for what appears to be a long time and was near death at one point. Why didn't God heal him earlier in his sickness?

_____
_____

** What lessons can be drawn from this passage regarding divine healing?_____

_____

Philippians 2:28-30 *Therefore I have sent him all the more eagerly so that when you see him again you may rejoice and I may be less concerned [about you].* **29** *Receive him then in the Lord with all joy, and hold men like him in high regard;* **30** *because he came close to death for the work of Christ, risking his life to complete what was deficient in your service to me.*

TQ: ** What further information are we given about Epaphroditus?_____

_____

** Why was the church to receive him with joy?_____

_____

DQ: ** What was deficient in the church's service to Paul?_____

_____

** How would they hold Epaphroditus in high regard?_____

_____

A-6   The Compass Paul Followed -- Philippians 3:1-21

B-1   Paul's Compass Described -- Philippians 3:1-14

Philippians 3:1-3   *Finally, my brethren, rejoice in the Lord. To write the same things [again] is no trouble to me, and it is a safeguard for you.* **2** *Beware of the dogs, beware of the evil workers, beware of the false circumcision;* **3** *for we are the [true] circumcision, who worship in the Spirit of God and glory in Christ Jesus and put no confidence in the flesh,*

FYI: **Dogs** (Gk. *kuon*) -- Literally, *dog*; figuratively, a term of reproach for persons regarded as *unholy, imprudent, impure*.

The **false circumcision** were Judaizers who insisted the Gentiles must become Jews, or at least obedient to the law, before they could become Christians. Acts 15 records the "minutes" of the church council when this issue was decided. Paul wrote the letter to the Galatians to combat this heresy.

TQ: ** What did Paul mention as the components of the "true circumcision"?

_____

_____

** Discuss and explain each of these three concepts.

_____

_____

Philippians 3:4-6   *although I myself might have confidence even in the flesh. If anyone else has a mind to put confidence in the flesh, I far more:* **5** *circumcised the eighth day, of the nation of Israel, of the tribe of Benjamin, a Hebrew of Hebrews; as to the Law, a Pharisee;* **6** *as to zeal, a persecutor of the church; as to the righteousness which is in the Law, found blameless.*

FYI: **Flesh** has several nuances of meaning in the New Testament. When it is used in a negative sense, as here, it is contrasting the abilities or achievements of the physical person who follows the desires of his body and soul instead of the desires of his spirit. (See Glossary: *Flesh*.)

See 2 Corinthians 11:18-33 for a related list.

DQ: ** Paul listed several things that he considers to be flesh. Look behind the surface details and name the categories that Paul considered flesh.

_____

** Jewish circumcision is a religious ritual. What religious rituals do Christians regard highly?_____

** Are they flesh as well?_____
** Explain._____

Philippians 3:7-8   _But whatever things were gain to me, those things I have counted as loss for the sake of Christ. **8** More than that, I count all things to be loss in view of the surpassing value of knowing Christ Jesus my Lord, for whom I have suffered the loss of all things, and count them but rubbish so that I may gain Christ,_

TQ: ** What had more value to Paul than all his earthly accomplishments?

_____

DQ: ** How would you describe this driving mission on Paul's compass?

_____

Philippians 3:9-11   _and may be found in Him, not having a righteousness of my own derived from [the] Law, but that which is through faith in Christ, the righteousness which [comes] from God on the basis of faith, **10** that I may know Him and the power of His resurrection and the fellowship of His sufferings, being conformed to His death; **11** in order that I may attain to the resurrection from the dead._

TQ: ** What kind of righteousness did Paul reject?_____

** What kind did he want?_____

** What did Paul identify as his compass heading or guiding light in this passage?_____

** What goal did he ultimately have in mind?_____
_____

DQ: **Explain your understanding of Paul's goals._____
_____

** What have you chosen for your compass heading, your guiding light?
_____
_____

** To what end or goal?_____
_____

Philippians 3:12-14   *Not that I have already obtained [it] or have already become perfect, but I press on so that I may lay hold of that for which also I was laid hold of by Christ Jesus.* **13** *Brethren, I do not regard myself as having laid hold of [it] yet; but one thing [I do]: forgetting what [lies] behind and reaching forward to what [lies] ahead,* **14** *I press on toward the goal for the prize of the upward call of God in Christ Jesus.*

TQ: ** What did Paul say about his motivation in this passage?_____
_____

** Had Paul achieved God's purpose for his life at the time he wrote this letter?_____
_____

** What did he press on toward?_____
_____

DQ: ** What does "pressing toward" mean?_____
_____

** What was "behind" that Paul set aside to forget?_____
_____

** What was ahead for Paul that he reached toward?_____
_____

** What was the prize he was working to win?_____
_____

** What will you set aside and forget from your past?_____
_____

** What will you reach for?_____
_____

B-2 Paul's Compass Applied -- Philippians 3:15-21

Philippians 3:15-17   *Let us therefore, as many as are perfect, have this attitude; and if in anything you have a different attitude, God will reveal that also to you;* **16** *however, let us keep living by that same [standard] to which we have attained.* **17** *Brethren, join in following my example, and observe those who walk according to the pattern you have in us.*

FYI: Most of us shy away from thinking of ourselves as perfect. Paul's reference, though, isn't to absolute perfection, but to a level of maturity consistent with one's growth and experience. A 5 year old can be "perfect" as a 5 year old, but immature compared to a teenager. This attitude is the mark of one who is acting in proper maturity, regardless of age.

TQ: ** What attitude are we to have?_____
_____

DQ: ** What does he mean about living by the standard to which we have attained?_____
_____
** Does this rule out improving our standard of living?_____
** Explain your answer._____
_____

Philippians 3:18-19   *For many walk, of whom I often told you, and now tell you even weeping, [that they are] enemies of the cross of Christ,* **19** *whose end is destruction, whose god is [their] appetite, and [whose] glory is in their shame, who set their minds on earthly things.*

TQ: ** How can we recognize "enemies of the cross"?_____
_____

DQ: ** Could these enemies of the cross be in the church?_____
** Explain._____
_____
** What would "friends of the cross" be like?_____
_____

Philippians 3:20-21 *For our citizenship is in heaven, from which also we eagerly wait for a Savior, the Lord Jesus Christ;* **21** *who will transform the body of our humble state into conformity with the body of His glory, by the exertion of the power that He has even to subject all things to Himself.*

FYI: This passage would be a great encouragement to a church that was struggling with political opposition and persecution. Paul is essentially showing them a guiding light at the end of a dark tunnel (Philippians 3:11).

For a more comprehensive discussion of the importance of the resurrection and a description of the resurrected body, read 1 Corinthians 15. (See Glossary: *Resurrection.*)

TQ: ** What will Christ do?_____

_____

** How will it get done?_____

_____

DQ: ** Where is Jesus that we must wait for Him?_____

_____

** What does this mean?_____

_____

** Since He has the power to subject all things to Himself, why doesn't He do it?_____

_____

** Explain how this letter would help believers maximize their rewards and benefits in the resurrection and the Judgment Seat of Christ.

_____

_____

A-7 Greetings and Final Thoughts – Philippians 4:1-23

Philippians 4:1 *Therefore, my beloved brethren whom I long [to see], my joy and crown, in this way stand firm in the Lord, my beloved.*

TQ: ** What is the "therefore" there for?_____

_____

DQ: ** How would the church be Paul's joy and crown?_____

_____

** In what way do we stand firm in the Lord?_____

Philippians 4:2-3   *I urge Euodia and I urge Syntyche to live in harmony in the Lord. **3** Indeed, true companion, I ask you also to help these women who have shared my struggle in [the cause of] the gospel, together with Clement also and the rest of my fellow workers, whose names are in the book of life.*

FYI: **Euodia** (*"success"* or perhaps *"fragrant"*)
        Syntyche (*"happy event"*)
        Clement (*"mild, merciful"*)

TQ: ** How are Euodia and Syntyche associated with Paul?_____

        ** What seems to be their problem?_____

        ** What has Clement been doing?_____

        ** What does it mean that their names are in the book of life?_____

Philippians 4:4-5   *Rejoice in the Lord always; again I will say, rejoice! **5** Let your gentle [spirit] be known to all men. The Lord is near.*

TQ: ** How would one make known, or demonstrate, a gentle spirit?

DQ: ** The church was in the midst of persecution and Paul was in prison. What were they to rejoice over?_____

        ** Explain how the Lord can be near when we are awaiting His return from heaven (Philippians 3:20)._____

Philippians 4:6-7   *Be anxious for nothing, but in everything by prayer and supplication with thanksgiving let your requests be made known to God. **7** And the peace of God,* *which surpasses all comprehension, will guard your hearts and your minds in Christ Jesus.*

FYI: This would be a good passage to memorize.

TQ: ** What process does Paul describe for getting rid of anxiety?

_____

_____

DQ: ** In what way does peace guard your hearts and minds?_____

_____

Philippians 4:8 *Finally, brethren, whatever is true, whatever is honorable, whatever is right, whatever is pure, whatever is lovely, whatever is of good repute, if there is any excellence and if anything worthy of praise, dwell on these things.*

FYI: **True** (Gk. *alethes*) – Statements that agree with the facts, things that are characterized by reality: *true, genuine, real, trustworthy, honest.*

Honorable (Gk. *semnos*) – That which calls forth honor, veneration and respect from others: *honorable, of good character, worthy of respect, noble.*

Right (Gk. *dikaios*) -- Morally and ethically righteous, *upright, just, law abiding, fair, proper.*

Pure (Gk. *hagnos*) – Characterized by moral purity: *pure, free from sin, innocent, blameless, acceptable.*

Lovely (Gk. *prosphiles*) -- What is pleasing, *acceptable, lovely, friendly.*

Of good repute (Gk. *euphemos*) – Praiseworthy, *commendable, having a good report.*

Excellence (Gk. *arete*) – Having a good quality of any kind: *excellence, goodness, valor, virtue, uprightness.*

Worthy of praise (Gk. *epainos*) -- An expression of high evaluation: *praise, approval, commendation.*

DQ: ** Why would Paul want us to think on these things?_____

_____

Philippians 4:9 *The things you have learned and received and heard and seen in me, practice these things, and the God of peace will be with you.*

TQ: ** What was the church supposed to do?_____
_____

DQ: ** Do you have a role model that you are imitating (1 Corinthians 11:1, Hebrews 6:12, 13:7)?_____

** Are you a role model for others to imitate?_____
_____

Philippians 4:10-11 *But I rejoiced in the Lord greatly, that now at last you have revived your concern for me; indeed, you were concerned [before], but you lacked opportunity.* **11** *Not that I speak from want, for I have learned to be content in whatever circumstances I am.*

FYI: Paul was very gracious in his dealing with the churches. The Philippian church was the only church that helped him in his missionary journeys (verse 15). Even when they were doing nothing, he provided an excuse for their neglect. Paul had no expectations of the churches for his support, he purposed to minister without charging for his services (Acts 18:3, 1 Corinthians 9:16-18, 2 Corinthians 11:7).

Paul did not have the Western mindset of pursuing more money, possessions or personal comfort. Psalm 23:1 is another statement of contentment. Sometimes we must just set our will not to want or desire anything other than what God provides for us.

DQ: ** What lesson did Paul learn?_____

** How do you suppose he learned it?_____
_____

Philippians 4:12-13 *I know how to get along with humble means, and I also know how to live in prosperity; in any and every circumstance I have learned the secret of being filled and going hungry, both of having abundance and suffering need.* **13** *I can do all things through Him who strengthens me.*

TQ: ** What was Paul's secret for contentment?_____
_____

DQ: ** Are you satisfied and content with your situation?_____
** Explain._____
_____

Philippians 4:14-16   *Nevertheless, you have done well to share [with me] in my affliction.* **15** *You yourselves also know, Philippians, that at the first preaching of the gospel, after I left Macedonia, no church shared with me in the matter of giving and receiving but you alone;* **16** *for even in Thessalonica you sent [a gift] more than once for my needs.*

TQ: ** What did the Philippian church do?_____

_____

DQ: ** Would you characterize your support of missionaries and other gospel workers as being like the Philippians, or one of the other churches?_____

_____

Philippians 4:17-19   *Not that I seek the gift itself, but I seek for the profit which increases to your account.* **18** *But I have received everything in full and have an abundance; I am amply supplied, having received from Epaphroditus what you have sent, a fragrant aroma, an acceptable sacrifice, well-pleasing to God.* **19** *And my God will supply all your needs according to His riches in glory in Christ Jesus.*

FYI: The sacrifice involved in sending money to Paul was seen as a good and pleasing thing, not only to Paul, but to God. The reference to a fragrant aroma shows that God saw the sacrifice and was pleased with it (Exodus 29:18, Ephesians 5:2).
Verse 19 is another good verse to memorize.

TQ: ** What comes to those who help gospel workers?_____

_____

** What had Epaphroditus done?_____

_____

** Where are our accounts kept safe?_____

_____

DQ: ** When will they be dispensed?_____

_____

** What is the profit that "increases to your account"?_____

_____

Philippians 4:20-22   *Now to our God and Father [be] the glory for-ever and ever. Amen.* **21** *Greet every saint in Christ Jesus. The brethren who are with me greet you.* **22** *All the saints greet you, especially those of Caesar's household.*

TQ: ** Who is being greeted by whom?_____

_____

Philippians 4:23   *The grace of the Lord Jesus Christ be with your spirit.*

DQ: ** How would this blessing affect their lives?_____

_____

RECAP: Paul mentions several key goals that defined his mission or "compass heading." Review this letter, then identify and explain them all here.

_____
_____
_____
_____
_____
_____
_____
_____
_____
_____
_____
_____
_____
_____

Describe the compass heading that guides your own life._____

_____
_____
_____
_____
_____
_____

Colossians: A Study Guide for LIFE

Outline and Table of Contents

Background Information

Author:　The Apostle Paul (Colossians 1:1). He wrote this letter to the people of Colossae, a city situated in the same valley as Laodicea (Colossians 4:15-16) in the area called Phrygia in the Roman province of Asia.

Date:　The letter was written during Paul's imprisonment in Rome (Acts 28), probably 62-63 AD.

Theme:　The purpose of the letter was to explain and exalt the person of the Lord Jesus Christ. In doing this, he also dealt with four heresies or problem areas that were invading the early church.

1. The worship of angels (Colossians 2:18).
2. The cult known as the Gnostics (based on *gnosis*, the Greek word for knowledge). The Gnostics brought elements from other forms of worship together in a belief that they had the true knowledge of spiritual life. They were similar to the new age movement of today. (Note Paul's emphasis on true knowledge in Colossians 1:9-10, 2:2-3 and 3:10.)
3. False doctrines, such as the belief that there were gods (called the demiurge) between God and man who created and maintained the material universe. (See Colossians 1:16-17, 2:8.)
4. Astrology and similar philosophies from various superstitions and false worship. (See Colossians 2:9, 16-23.)

The church in Colossae had trouble with the Gnostics; in Galatia, the church was influenced by the Judaizers. Paul's solution to both of these problems was to refocus the churches' attention on the person of the Lord Jesus Christ (Galatians 1:6-7; Colossians 3:1-4).

Colossians: A Study Guide for LIFE

A-1 Salutation – Colossians 1:1-2

Colossians 1:1-2   *Paul, an apostle of Jesus Christ by the will of God, and Timothy our brother, 2 To the saints and faithful brethren in Christ [who are] at Colossae: Grace to you and peace from God our Father.*

TQ: ** Who sent this letter?_____
           ** To whom was it written?_____
           _____
           ** What blessing did he give them?_____
           _____
           ** What did he say about himself?_____
           _____

A-2 Paul Thanks God – Colossians 1:3-14

Colossians 1:3-5   *We give thanks to God, the Father of our Lord Jesus Christ, praying always for you, 4 since we heard of your faith in Christ Jesus and the love which you have for all the saints; 5 because of the hope laid up for you in heaven, of which you previously heard in the word of truth, the gospel*

FYI: **Faith** (Gk. *pistis*) – *Trust, belief, conviction.* Faith is the single-minded pursuit of God's plan and purposes.
           Love (Gk. agapao) – *A self-sacrificing, non-emotional act that seeks the best for another person.*
           Hope (Gk. *elpis*) – Firm confidence and expectation that what God has promised He will fully accomplish: *hope.*

TQ: ** Paul valued the three virtues: faith, hope and love (1 Corinthians 13:13). In what context are these virtues mentioned in this passage?
           _____
           _____

** What caused Paul's thanksgiving?_____

_____

DQ: ** Why do you suppose these virtues have the highest value?

_____

** What virtues are most valuable in your opinion?_____

_____

Colossians 1:6-8   *which has come to you, just as in all the world also it is constantly bearing fruit and increasing, even as [it has been doing] in you also since the day you heard [of it] and understood the grace of God in truth;* **7** *just as you learned [it] from Epaphras, our beloved fellow bond-servant, who is a faithful servant of Christ on our behalf,* **8** *and he also informed us of your love in the Spirit.*

FYI: **Epaphras** (*"lovely"*)

Paul is famous for writing long and involved sentences. Go back to the prior passage and read the first half of this sentence to follow the details of what he is saying.

TQ: ** What was bearing fruit and increasing?_____

** Who first brought the message to the church?_____

** What does this passage suggest of his activities?_____

** What do we know of Epaphras from this passage?_____

_____

Colossians 1:9   *For this reason also, since the day we heard [of it], we have not ceased to pray for you and to ask that you may be filled with the knowledge of His will in all spiritual wisdom and understanding,*

FYI: Begin now to separately identify every reference to the Father, the Son and the Holy Spirit in this epistle. Highlighting each name and pronoun with a different colored pencil for each Person is very effective, but you could also put letters ("F," "J," or "HS") over each reference.

TQ: ** What was Paul's prayer for the church?_____

_____

DQ: ** What does it mean "to be filled with the knowledge of His will"?

_____

_____

** Does this describe you?_____

** What is the difference between _spiritual wisdom_ (wisdom of the spirit) and _understanding_?_____

_____

Colossians 1:10-12   _so that you will walk in a manner worthy of the Lord, to please [Him] in all respects, bearing fruit in every good work and increasing in the knowledge of God;_ **11** _strengthened with all power, according to His glorious might, for the attaining of all steadfastness and patience; joyously_ **12** _giving thanks to the Father, who has qualified us to share in the inheritance of the saints in Light._

TQ: ** Examine his entire prayer (1:9-12) and carefully distinguish the requests from the desired results. What does he ask for?_____

_____

** What results does he expect his prayer to produce?_____

_____

DQ: ** What would "worthy walk" involve?_____

_____

** What is the fruit that we should be bearing?_____

_____

** How can you increase your experiences with God?_____

_____

** What do you expect your inheritance to include?_____

_____

** Are the results Paul mentioned evident in your life?_____

_____

Colossians 1:13-14   _For He rescued us from the domain of darkness, and transferred us to the kingdom of His beloved Son,_ **14** _in whom we have redemption, the forgiveness of sins._

FYI: **Domain** (Gk. _exousia_) – _Power to act, authority._ (The English term _domain_ means the area or territory in which a ruler or government exerts its authority.)

Kingdom (Gk. *basileia*) – *Royal power, kingship, dominion, rule.* (See Glossary.)

Redemption (See Glossary.)

TQ: ** Where were we?_____

_____

** Where are we now?_____

_____

** What happened?_____

_____

** Where is our forgiveness found?_____

_____

DQ: ** Explain what we were redeemed from._____

_____

** What made our redemption possible?_____

_____

** Satan has a domain; Jesus has a kingdom. What do you suppose the difference is?_____

_____

A-3   The Supremacy of Christ – Colossians 1:15-23

Colossians 1:15-17   *He is the image of the invisible God, the firstborn of all creation.* **16** *For by Him all things were created, [both] in the heavens and on earth, visible and invisible, whether thrones or dominions or rulers or authorities-- all things have been created through Him and for Him.* **17** *He is before all things, and in Him all things hold together.*

FYI: **Firstborn** (Gk. *prototokos:* the oldest son in the family) -- Jesus is the firstborn of all creation. This does NOT mean that Jesus was a created being. He is the creator, not part of the creation (Colossians 1:16). Being the firstborn speaks of His preeminence and importance as the One having all the rights, privileges and respect that typically go to the firstborn; namely, the right of inheritance, rulership, dominion, possessor, owner and supremacy. Jesus is spoken of as the firstborn in Romans 8:29; Colossians 1:15, 18; Hebrews 1:6, 12:23 and Revelation 1:5.

TQ: ** List the conceptual pictures that describe Christ in these verses.

_____

_____

** What does this passage say about Who created all things?_____

** Why were all things created?_____

Colossians 1:18 *He is also head of the body, the church; and He is the beginning, the firstborn from the dead, so that He Himself will come to have first place in everything.*

FYI: As **firstborn from the dead**, Jesus was the first to be resurrected from the dead to receive a glorified body. As a good shepherd, He goes before His flock to lead the way. Other people have come back from the dead, but they were only healed or resuscitated, not resurrected. They would have continued to live until they died a second time (1 Kings 17:17-24, 2 Kings 13:21, John 11:38-44).

TQ: ** What does this passage tell us about Christ?_____

DQ: ** How is Christ's headship manifested in the church?_____

** Is asking His blessing on our programs enough?_____
** Explain._____

** What does it mean that Christ holds all things together?_____

Colossians 1:19-20 *For it was the [Father's] good pleasure for all the fullness to dwell in Him, 20 and through Him to reconcile all things to Himself, having made peace through the blood of His cross; through Him, [I say], whether things on earth or things in heaven.*

FYI: Jesus completely illustrated and demonstrated who God is and what He is like. All of God's fullness lives in Jesus. (See John 1:14, 14:7-9; Hebrews 1:3.)

TQ: ** What can you add to your list of topics about Christ from this passage?_____

** How did He reconcile all things to himself?_____

DQ: ** What does it mean that God's fullness dwells in Christ?_____

** Since Christ is in us, do we have the fullness of God?_____

** Explain._____

Colossians 1:21-23 *And although you were formerly alienated and hostile in mind, [engaged] in evil deeds,* **22** *yet He has now reconciled you in His fleshly body through death, in order to present you before Him holy and blameless and beyond reproach—***23** *if indeed you continue in the faith firmly established and steadfast, and not moved away from the hope of the gospel that you have heard, which was proclaimed in all creation under heaven, and of which I, Paul, was made a minister.*

FYI: **Reconciliation:** See Glossary.
Sanctification: See Glossary.

TQ: ** What does this passage teach us about Christ?_____

** What is the end result of Christ's work in our lives?_____

** How did reconciliation take place?_____

** What is the central truth we must cling to (verse 23)?_____

DQ: ** What steps has God taken to reconcile you to Himself?_____

** What steps have you taken to be reconciled?_____

** What must we do to reach the intended end of God's process of reconciliation?_____

** Describe the hope of the gospel, the good news._____

A-4 Paul's Interest in the Colossians – Colossians 1:24-2:5

Colossians 1:24 *Now I rejoice in my sufferings for your sake, and in my flesh I do my share on behalf of His body, which*

> *is the church, in filling up what is lacking in Christ's afflictions.*

FYI: There was nothing lacking in Christ's work on the cross. Paul is referring to the current ongoing work of God in the body of Christ, the church. Paul's sufferings were for the sake of including the Gentiles in the body of Christ. They were an enormous group of people who had been excluded from the life of God until this time (Ephesians 2:12, 4:18). If Paul suffered for bringing Christ to the Gentiles, it was simply a minor factor compared to Christ's sufferings to make the inclusion of the Gentiles possible.

The church will experience the sufferings of life and the cross as Christ did (Romans 8:16-18). We should not expect to be carried to Heaven on flowery beds of ease.

TQ: ** Why does Paul rejoice in his suffering?_____

** Explain what is lacking in Christ's afflictions._____

DQ: ** The church in America has experienced a period of prosperity and peace. Do you see this as normal for the church or is this peace an unusual situation?_____

** What would you say is "normal" for the church living in this world? (See John 15:18-20; 16:33; James 1:2-4.)_____

Colossians 1:25-27 *Of [this church] I was made a minister according to the stewardship from God bestowed on me for your benefit, so that I might fully carry out the [preaching of] the word of God, **26** [that is], the mystery which has been hidden from the [past] ages and generations, but has now been manifested to His saints, **27** to whom God willed to make known what is the riches of the glory of this mystery among the Gentiles, which is Christ in you, the hope of glory.*

FYI: **Manifested** (Gk. *phaneroo*) – To make clear or visible, to become known.
Mystery: See Glossary.

TQ: ** What was Paul's stewardship?_____

** Explain what a biblical mystery is in your own words._____

** Explain the mystery Paul mentions in this passage._____

DQ: ** What does the "hope of glory" mean?_____

Colossians 1:28-29   *We proclaim Him, admonishing every man and teaching every man with all wisdom, so that we may present every man complete in Christ.* **29** *For this purpose also I labor, striving according to His power, which mightily works within me.*

TQ: ** Why did Paul labor?_____

** Is this different than what Christ was trying to do in verse 22?_____

DQ: ** Who was working, God or Paul?_____
** Explain._____

** What does "proclaiming Jesus" involve?_____

** Is your life proclaiming Jesus?_____

Colossians 2:1-3   *For I want you to know how great a struggle I have on your behalf and for those who are at Laodicea, and for all those who have not personally seen my face,* **2** *that their hearts may be encouraged, having been knit together in love, and [attaining] to all the wealth that comes from the full assurance of understanding, [resulting] in a true knowledge of God's mystery, [that is], Christ [Himself],* **3** *in whom are hidden all the treasures of wisdom and knowledge.*

TQ: ** Where are God's treasures found?_____

** What treasures did he mention in this passage?_____

DQ: ** What do you think Paul's struggle was?_____

** What treasures are you seeking?_____

** Where are you looking?_____

_____

Colossians 2:4-5   *I say this so that no one will delude you with persuasive argument.* **5** *For even though I am absent in body, nevertheless I am with you in spirit, rejoicing to see your good discipline and the stability of your faith in Christ.*

TQ: ** What would the "persuasive arguments" be intended to prove?_____

** What advice does he give that would prevent delusion from these arguments?_____

** What components of their lives did Paul see as being beneficial to their Christian walk?_____

_____

A-5 Fullness of Life in Christ – Colossians 2:6-15

Colossians 2:6-7   *Therefore as you have received Christ Jesus the Lord, [so] walk in Him,* **7** *having been firmly rooted [and now] being built up in Him and established in your faith, just as you were instructed, [and] overflowing with gratitude.*

TQ: ** What did he tell them to do?_____

** What has equipped or enabled them to do it?_____

DQ: ** How did you receive Christ?_____

** What does this tell you about how to walk in Him?_____

** The verbs "firmly rooted," "built up," "established," and "instructed" are all passive; that is, they happened to us, but we didn't actively create the result. Can you identify when and how these things happened to you?_____

_____

** Are they still happening?_____

_____

Colossians 2:8-9   *See to it that no one takes you captive through philosophy and empty deception, according to the tradition of men, according to the elementary principles of the world, rather than according to Christ. **9** For in Him all the fullness of Deity dwells in bodily form,*

TQ: ** What did Paul warn us against in this passage?_____

_____

** What principles are we to live by?_____

_____

** What does this passage tell us about Christ?_____

_____

DQ: ** What elementary principles of your culture conflict with the truth of God's Word, the Bible?_____

_____

** What do you believe and practice that are contrary to Biblical principles ?_____

_____

** What is the basis for what you believe?_____

_____

Colossians 2:10-12   *and in Him you have been made complete, and He is the head over all rule and authority; **11** and in Him you were also circumcised with a circumcision made without hands, in the removal of the body of the flesh by the circumcision of Christ; **12** having been buried with Him in baptism, in which you were also raised up with Him through faith in the working of God, who raised Him from the dead.*

FYI: **Made without hands** is a phrase that indicates the topic deals with spiritual realities, not physical or fleshly ones.

Circumcision was required of Abraham and his descendants to be a sign and a physical reminder that they were members of the everlasting covenant God made with Abraham (Genesis 17:1-14).

The body of the flesh is equivalent to the "old self" (Colossians

3:9) which refers to our old manner of life when we lived for our own fleshly desires instead for Christ.

Are you identifying the pronouns (He, Him) that refer to the members of the Godhead in every section?

TQ: ** How have we been made complete?_____
_____
_____

** What had happened to us as a result of believing in Christ?
_____
_____

** What is Paul's central message in this passage?_____
_____

Colossians 2:13-14 *When you were dead in your transgressions and the uncircumcision of your flesh, He made you alive together with Him, having forgiven us all our transgressions,* **14** *having canceled out the certificate of debt consisting of decrees against us, which was hostile to us; and He has taken it out of the way, having nailed it to the cross.*

FYI: If we were to think of God creating a warrant for our arrest every time we sinned or did something against His will, we would begin to understand the certificates of debt and the degrees God holds against us. Each of these "warrants" carries the penalty of eternal death (Ezekiel 18:4, 20). These were the certificates that were, in effect, nailed to the cross of Christ to indicate the reasons for Christ's death. (The actual "certificate" is described in John 19:19-20.) Paul is describing the legal framework that enables God to transfer our sins to the cross to be paid by means of Christ's death. This idea isn't literal, but it accurately describes how God is able to be both just and the justifier to those who believe in Christ (Romans 3:26).

TQ: ** Identify the pronouns; who made you alive?_____
_____

** What was your condition before you came to Christ?_____
_____

** What happened in the spiritual realm when you believed?_____
_____

Colossians 2:15   *When He had disarmed the rulers and authorities, He made a public display of them, having triumphed over them through Him.*

FYI: The **rulers** *and* **authorities** refer to the demonic authorities led by satan. He is alluding to the practice of victorious generals in the Roman army who would humiliate the leaders of the conquered nations in their victory celebrations.

TQ: ** What did the cross accomplish?_____

_____

DQ: ** What actual power does satan now have? (1 Peter 3:14 provides a hint to the correct answer.)_____

_____

A-6   Living in Victory over Sin – Colossians 2:16-3:17

Colossians 2:16-17   *Therefore no one is to act as your judge in regard to food or drink or in respect to a festival or a new moon or a Sabbath day—17 things which are a [mere] shadow of what is to come; but the substance belongs to Christ.*

FYI: This passage is an indication that New Testament believers are no longer under the Jewish regulations governing the feasts, dietary restrictions, special days or the Sabbath.

TQ: ** What is the "therefore" there for?_____

** Why are Christians no longer under those regulations?

_____

_____

DQ: ** Explain what Paul means regarding "shadow" and "substance" in this passage._____

** What do you suppose "the substance belongs to Christ" means?

_____

_____

Colossians 2:18-19   *Let no one keep defrauding you of your prize by delighting in self-abasement and the worship of the angels, taking his stand on [visions] he has seen, inflated* *without cause by his fleshly mind, **19** and not holding fast to the head, from whom the entire body, being supplied and held together by the joints and ligaments, grows with a growth which is from God.*

FYI: **Defraud** (Gk. *katabrabeuo*) – *Of an umpire: to decide against, disqualify from winning, judge unworthy.*

Self-abasement (Gk. *tapeinophrosune*) – Having a humble opinion of one's self, a deep sense of one's (moral) littleness: *modesty, humility, lowliness of mind*. It is used in this verse in a negative sense to indicate false humility and self-humiliation or mortification of the body.

Paul had unusual experiences in God, but he didn't "inflate himself without cause by his fleshly mind." A good example of how he treated seeing a vision (or having the actual experience) of being in Paradise is found in 2 Corinthians 12:1-10.

A **fleshly mind** is a mind that is set on the things of the flesh (the desires of the body and the soul) not the spirit. (See Glossary: *Flesh*.)

Body: See Glossary.
Soul: See Glossary.

TQ: ** How could we be defrauded out of our prize?_____

_____

** What does Paul consider to be more important than self-abasement and seeing visions?_____

_____

** Since Christ is the head, what is the body?_____

_____

DQ: ** What are the joints and ligaments of this body?_____

_____

** What work do they do in the church?_____

_____

** How does one "hold fast to the head"?_____

_____

** What is a fleshly mind?_____

_____

** Explain how the joints and ligaments work to cause growth in the spiritual body of the church._____

_____

Colossians 2:20-22   *If you have died with Christ to the elementary principles of the world, why, as if you were living in the world, do you submit yourself to decrees, such as, **21** "Do* *not handle, do not taste, do not touch!" 22 (which all [re-fer] [to] things destined to perish with use)-- in accor-dance with the commandments and teachings of men?*

FYI: **Elementary principles** (Gk. *stoicheion*) – Literally, a small upright post; figuratively, the first beginning, element or principle. Generally, the rudimentary elements of anything or what belongs to a basic series in any field of knowledge: in grammar, the ABCs; in speech, basic sounds; in physics, the four basic elements (earth, air, fire, water); in geometry, the axioms. As used in the New Testament: *elementary doctrines, fun-damental teachings, basic principles, binding traditions, taboos, prohi-bitions, ceremonies.*
World: See Glossary.

TQ: ** Explain the believer's relationship to the elementary principles of the world. _____

_____
** What are the rules the flesh devises to control sinful behavior?

_____
_____
** What did Paul say about these rules?_____

_____

Colossians 2:23 *These are matters which have, to be sure, the appearance of wisdom in self-made religion and self--abasement and severe treatment of the body, [but are] of no value against fleshly indulgence.*

FYI: There is an unfortunate chapter break after this passage. If you stop studying now, you only see what doesn't work to break the hold of sin. Do yourself a favor and keep reading to the end of this section.

TQ: ** How logical are these rules?_____

_____
** What is the spiritual reality of them?_____

_____

Colossians 3:1 *Therefore if you have been raised up with Christ, keep seeking the things above, where Christ is, seated at the right hand of God. 2 Set your mind on the things above, not on the things that are on earth.*

TQ: ** What is the "therefore" there for?_____

_____

** Instead of being concerned with rules that try to restrict our behaviors, what should we do?_____

_____

DQ: ** How do we seek the things above?_____

** Give examples of setting your mind on the things on earth._____

_____

** Give examples of setting our minds on things above._____

_____

Colossians 3:3-4

For you have died and your life is hidden with Christ in God. 4 When Christ, who is our life, is revealed, then you also will be revealed with Him in glory.

FYI: **Life** (2x) (Gk. *zoe*) – See Glossary.

In times of personal revival, our minds are naturally centered in Christ; we have no struggle against sin. The key to victory is not found in rules or laws, but in keeping our minds and thinking focused and centered on Christ.

DQ: ** Explain how you have died. (Romans 6 discusses this in length.)

_____

_____

** Explain how and when our lives are hidden in Christ, _____

_____

** When will our lives be revealed with Him?_____

_____

Colossians 3:5-7

Therefore consider the members of your earthly body as dead to immorality, impurity, passion, evil desire, and greed, which amounts to idolatry. 6 For it is because of these things that the wrath of God will come upon the sons of disobedience, 7 and in them you also once walked, when you were living in them.

FYI: **Immorality** (Gk. *porneia*) – Every kind of extramarital, unlawful or unnatural sexual intercourse: *fornication, sexual immorality, prostitution.*

Impurity (Gk. *akatharsia*) – *Worthless material, waste; uncleanness, defilement, moral uncleanness or impurity.*

Passion (Gk. *pathos*) – A strong emotion of desire or craving, uncontrolled sexual passion: *lustful desire, evil craving.*

Evil desire (Gk. *epithumia*) – An unrestrained desire for something forbidden: *lust craving, evil desire.*

Greed (Gk. *pleonexia*) – A disposition of wanting more than one's share: *greed, covetousness.*

Idolatry (Gk. *eidololatria*) – The worship of idols or images.

Paul is applying the principles of this section to sinful behavior. Our bodies are tools that enable us to do God's will, yet they have desires that will lead us away from God. His advice is to keep your thinking on Christ, but to ignore (and resist) the demands and desires of your body as though it were dead.

TQ: ** What instructions did Paul explain in this passage?_____
_____

** Why would God express His anger on unbelievers?_____
_____

** What would be the effect of considering your members dead to these activities?_____
_____

DQ: ** How are you and your friends doing on following Paul's instructions in this passage?_____
_____

** Is there a noticeable change for the better in the way you live now, and before you came to Christ?_____
_____

Colossians 3:8-11   *But now you also, put them all aside: anger, wrath, malice, slander, [and] abusive speech from your mouth.* **9** *Do not lie to one another, since you laid aside the old self with its [evil] practices,* **10** *and have put on the new self who is being renewed to a true knowledge according to the image of the One who created him—* **11** *[a renewal] in which there is no [distinction between] Greek and Jew, circumcised and uncircumcised, barbarian, Scythian, slave and freeman, but Christ is all, and in all.*

FYI: **Anger** (Gk. *orge*) – A vigorous upsurge of one's nature against someone or something: *anger, wrath, indignation.* (*Orge* is translated "wrath" in verse 6.)

Wrath (Gk. *thumos*) -- Anger that boils up and subsides again, hot temper: *angry outburst, wrath, rage.*

Malice (Gk. *kakia*) – Having the quality of evil: *moral depravity, vice, wickedness, ill will, hatefulness.*

Slander (Gk. *blasphemia*) -- Harmful and abusive speech against someone's reputation: *slander, reviling, evil speaking.*

Abusive speech (Gk. *aischrologia*) -- Dirty talk, filthy or obscene language or speech.

Barbarian (Gk. *barbaros*) -- One speaking a strange speech or foreign language, being non-Greek in language and culture: *uncivilized, barbarian.*

Scythian (Gk. *skuthes*) -- An inhabitant of Scythia, considered to be the wildest of the barbarians. Scythia is located in modern southern Russia

The references to the old self or the new self (the King James Version accurately translates this as the old or new *man*) are to the behavior a believer had before and after becoming a Christian. The old self followed the dictates of the body and the soul. The new self follows the direction of the Holy Spirit in our human spirits. Putting on the new man is equivalent to putting on Christ (Romans 13:14).

TQ: ** Identify the behaviors we are to put aside or stop doing.

_____

** What do these behaviors have in common?_____

** What did Paul assume happens when a person becomes a Christian?_____

** What is to happen to the new self when it is activated or put on?

_____

DQ: ** Are these conditions true for you?_____

** In Christ, what distinctions remain between groups of people?_____

** What broad categories of humanity can you distinguish in verse 11?

_____

Colossians 3:12-13   *So, as those who have been chosen of God, holy and beloved, put on a heart of compassion, kindness, humility, gentleness and patience;* **13** *bearing with one another, and forgiving each other, whoever has a com-*

plaint against anyone; just as the Lord forgave you, so also should you.

FYI: God has sovereignly determined to reject all of man's effort to please Him. (These efforts are known as "religion.") No matter how expensive the sacrifice or strong the motivation of the person, his efforts will be rejected by God. God has, however, established that those who come to Him through Christ will be accepted. Christ made the one sacrifice in all the world that satisfied God's demands. From God's perspective, those who choose Christ are "chosen by God." Christ is our *propitiation*, the satisfying sacrifice (Romans 3:25, 1 John 2:2). (See Glossary: *Propitiation*.)

TQ: ** What behavior will be in evidence when one has put on the new self?
_____
_____
** What is implied if these behaviors are not in evidence?_____
_____

DQ: ** How do you know you have been chosen by God?_____
_____
** If you have been chosen by God, is putting on the new self optional?
_____
** Explain._____
_____
** Does your actual behavior reflect your old or new self?_____
_____

Colossians 3:14-15 *Beyond all these things [put on] love, which is the perfect bond of unity.* **15** *Let the peace of Christ rule in your hearts, to which indeed you were called in one body; and be thankful.*

FYI: **Love** (Gk. *agape*) – See Glossary.

TQ: ** What is the ultimate thing to put on?_____
_____
** How is its connection with unity?_____
_____
** Define love in your own words._____
_____
** How do we let peace rule?_____
_____

DQ: ** Would you be considered a hypocrite if you act out of love when you feel disgust or dislike?_____

** What defines who we really are: our behavior or our feelings?_____

** Explain._____

Colossians 3:16-17   *Let the word of Christ richly dwell within you, with all wisdom teaching and admonishing one another with psalms [and] hymns [and] spiritual songs, singing with thankfulness in your hearts to God. **17** Whatever you do in word or deed, [do] all in the name of the Lord Jesus, giving thanks through Him to God the Father.*

FYI: This would be better translated as; *"… with all wisdom be teaching and admonishing one another. With psalms [and] hymns [and] spiritual songs, be singing with thankfulness in your hearts to God."* (Ephesians 5:19 should be translated in a similar way.) The original manuscripts do not have punctuation marks.

TQ: ** What principle should guide and control our behaviors?_____

DQ: ** How have Christ's words been richly dwelling in you?

** What songs do you sing to yourself and God?_____

**'What does it mean to act in the name of the Lord?_____

A-7 Living Victoriously in Relationships -- Colossians 3:18-4:6

FYI: These verses are a summary of the complete instructions Paul gave in Ephesians 5:21-6:9. He wrote both Colossians and Ephesians (as well as Philippians and Philemon) during the time he was imprisoned in Rome.

Colossians 3:18   *Wives, be subject to your husbands, as is fitting in the Lord.*

FYI: Some husbands use this verse to domineer and subjugate their wives. The full instruction in Ephesians, however, clearly shows that there must be a mutual submission between husbands and wives.

DQ: ** Read Ephesians 5:21-33 and 1 Peter 3:1-7. List the new-self behaviors that are expected for the wife._____

Colossians 3:19 *Husbands, love your wives and do not be embittered against them.*

FYI: **Love** (Gk. *agapao*) – See Glossary.
Embittered (Gk. *pikraino*) -- To make bitter or undrinkable: *become angry, resentful.*

TQ: ** From your research in Ephesians 5:21-33 and 1 Peter 3:1-7 list the new-self behaviors that are expected for the husband._____

DQ: ** It is correctly said that men need respect and women need love (Ephesians 5:33), but we tend to treat others the way we want to be treated. Would it be possible for a wife to love her husband (the way *she* wants to be treated) without respecting him (the way *he* wants to be treated)?_____
** Explain._____

** Can a man respect his wife without loving her?_____
** Explain._____

** Why would a man be embittered against his wife?_____

** What is Paul's secret for husbands and wives to get along?_____

Colossians 3:20 *Children, be obedient to your parents in all things, for this is well-pleasing to the Lord.*

TQ: ** How are children to respond to their parents?_____

** Why are they to do that?_____

DQ: ** If children are not taught to be obedient to their parents, how will they respond to their Heavenly Father?_____

** Do you suppose a permissive society that encourages individuality and independence in children (leading to rebellion and self-centeredness) is part of satan's strategy for this world?_____
** Explain._____

** Do you exemplify obedience to God for your children or peers?_____

Colossians 3:21
Fathers, do not exasperate your children, so that they will not lose heart.

FYI: **Exasperate** (Gk. *erethizo*) -- *To stir to anger, make resentful, irritate.*

DQ: ** What would a father do that would exasperate his children?_____

** What does it mean "to lose heart"?_____

** How does your Heavenly Father discipline you?_____

Colossians 3:22-25
Slaves, in all things obey those who are your masters on earth, not with external service, as those who [merely] please men, but with sincerity of heart, fearing the Lord. 23 Whatever you do, do your work heartily, as for the Lord rather than for men, 24 knowing that from the Lord you will receive the reward of the inheritance. It is the Lord Christ whom you serve. 25 For he who does wrong will receive the consequences of the wrong which he has done, and that without partiality.

FYI: Instructions given to slaves in Paul's culture are also applicable to employees in today's culture. In the same way, instructions to masters are applicable to employers.

TQ: ** How is an employee supposed to work?_____

** Why?_____

** If our work pleases our bosses, we get paychecks. What do we get if our work pleases the Lord?_____

DQ: ** What would be the consequences from our bosses if we do wrong?
_____
_____

** What would be the consequences from the Lord?_____
_____

** How does your work ethic compare to these instructions?_____
_____

Colossians 4:1   *Masters, grant to your slaves justice and fairness, knowing that you too have a Master in heaven.*

TQ: ** How are employers supposed to act toward their employees?_____
_____

** What would be their motivation?_____
_____

Colossians 4:2-4   *Devote yourselves to prayer, keeping alert in it with [an attitude of] thanksgiving;* **3** *praying at the same time for us as well, that God will open up to us a door for the word, so that we may speak forth the mystery of Christ, for which I have also been imprisoned;* **4** *that I may make it clear in the way I ought to speak.*

TQ: ** How are we supposed to pray?_____
_____

** What does Paul ask prayer for?_____
_____

DQ: ** Do you think that praying for another person's health, wealth and happiness is the highest request we can make?_____
_____

** What would be a higher purpose?_____
_____

Colossians 4:5-6   *Conduct yourselves with wisdom toward outsiders, making the most of the opportunity.* **6** *Let your speech always be with grace, [as though] seasoned with salt, so that you will know how you should respond to each person.*

TQ: ** What is the goal or purpose of wisdom (wise conduct) in this passage?_____

** What are the guidelines Paul gave concerning the way we should witness for Christ?_____

DQ: ** What role does Paul expect each Christian to fulfill?_____

** Is this reasonable?_____ Explain._____

** Who are the outsiders?_____

** What is speech flavored by grace?_____

** What is the seasoning of salt?_____

A-8 Paul's Greetings -- Colossians 4:7-18

Colossians 4:7-9   *As to all my affairs, Tychicus, [our] beloved brother and faithful servant and fellow bond-servant in the Lord, will bring you information.* **8** *[For] I have sent him to you for this very purpose, that you may know about our circumstances and that he may encourage your hearts;* **9** *and with him Onesimus, [our] faithful and beloved brother, who is one of your [number]. They will inform you about the whole situation here.*

FYI: Paul didn't say much about **Onesimus** in this letter, but Onesimus was a slave who ran away from Philemon, the pastor of the church Paul started in Colossae. Onesimus found Paul in Rome and started helping him in prison. During this time, Onesimus gave his life to Christ (Philemon 1:10). Now, Paul is sending Onesimus back to Philemon, his former master. Tychicus is taking another letter in which Paul appeals to Philemon on behalf of Onesimus. The New Testament epistle to Philemon is a copy of Paul's appeal.

TQ: ** What does Paul tell us about Tychicus?_____

** What is his mission?_____

** What does he tell us about Onesimus?_____

_____

Colossians 4:10-11   *Aristarchus, my fellow prisoner, sends you his greetings; and [also] Barnabas's cousin Mark (about whom you received instructions; if he comes to you, welcome him); **11** and [also] Jesus who is called Justus; these are the only fellow workers for the kingdom of God who are from the circumcision, and they have proved to be an encouragement to me.*

FYI: **Aristarchus** (*"best ruler"* or *"best leader"*)
Barnabas (*"son of rest"*)
Mark (*"a defense"*)
Justus (*"just"*)

TQ: ** Identify and describe the other men who also sent greetings to the church._____

_____

** What did he say about these men as a group?_____

_____

DQ: ** If you were there, what would you want Paul to say about you?

_____

_____

** What do you think he would really say?_____

_____

Colossians 4:12-13   *Epaphras, who is one of your number, a bond-slave of Jesus Christ, sends you his greetings, always laboring earnestly for you in his prayers, that you may stand perfect and fully assured in all the will of God. **13** For I testify for him that he has a deep concern for you and for those who are in Laodicea and Hierapolis.*

FYI: **Epaphras** (*"lovely"*)
Laodicea (*"justice of the people"*) – a city of Phrygia, near Colossae.
Hierapolis (*"holy city'"*) -- a city of Phrygia, also near Colossae.
Find Colossae, Laodicea and Hierapolis in the maps at the back of your Bible.

TQ: ** Who is Epaphras?_____

_____

** How did he pray for the church in Colossae?_____

_____

** How did Paul pray for the church (Colossians 1:9-12)?_____

_____

DQ: ** How do you pray for others?_____

_____

Colossians 4:14-15   *Luke, the beloved physician, sends you his greetings, and [also] Demas.* **15** *Greet the brethren who are in Laodicea and also Nympha and the church that is in her house.*

FYI: **Luke** (*"light giving"*)
Demas (*"governor of the people"*)
Nympha (*"bridegroom"*) – Some manuscripts show this name as *Nymphas,* a man's name. (KJV, NKJ, YLT are based on these manuscripts.) Other manuscripts show it as *Nympha,* a woman's name (NASB, NIV, ESV, NLT).
This is the only verse in the Bible that tells us Luke's profession. Luke is the author of the gospel of Luke and the book of Acts. When the book of Acts records that "we" did something, Luke was present (for example, Acts 16:10, 20:6). He was a frequent companion with Paul on his missionary journeys and was with him in Rome while he was in prison.

Colossians 4:16   *When this letter is read among you, have it also read in the church of the Laodiceans; and you, for your part read my letter [that is coming] from Laodicea.*

FYI: The letter to the Laodiceans is no longer in existence, although it is believed by some to be the letter we know as the Letter to the Ephesians. The manuscripts we have of Ephesians have the name Ephesus (Ephesus 1:1) written in a different hand. Even though Paul worked in Ephesus for a number of years, there is not one mention of his friends in the city. These facts suggest that the letter of Ephesians was something like a circular letter intended to be read by churches in several cities.

TQ: ** For whom were these letters intended?_____

_____

DQ: ** Do you ever hear these letters being read in your church?_____

** Should they be?_____

Colossians 4:17   *Say to Archippus, "Take heed to the ministry which you have received in the Lord, that you may fulfill it."*

FYI: **Archippus** (Gk. *archippos*) – Literally, horse-ruler, war horse, (in Philemon 1:2, Archippus is called a fellow soldier, a play on the meaning of his name.)

Many Christians seem to be at a loss to know what their ministry is. If this is the case for you, volunteer to help others in your church who have different tasks to perform. Try to do everything and learn every task: witness, help others, write your thoughts down, sing, teach others what you know, preach and pray for others. If something appeals to you or you have success in it, learn how to do it better. Be busy doing the things of the Lord. In the doing, you will soon learn your ministry. Even God can't guide a bicycle that leans against the wall.

DQ: ** We don't know Archippus' ministry, but since these instructions apply to us, what is your ministry in the Lord?_____

** Are you doing your best to fulfill it?_____

Colossians 4:18   *I, Paul, write this greeting with my own hand. Remember my imprisonment. Grace be with you.*

FYI: Since only about 5% of the population in Paul's day were literate (95% could neither read nor write), scribes were employed to write (and read) letters such as this. Paul was literate and wrote the concluding statements at least here and in 1 Corinthians 16:21.

DQ: ** How would they "remember" his imprisonment?_____

** What would they do?_____

** What does the concluding blessing mean?_____

RECAP: List the facts about Christ that Paul mentions in this letter._____

_____
_____
_____
_____
_____
_____
_____
_____
_____
_____
_____

What behaviors are believers expected to initiate and control; that is, what are they expected to "put on"? List them all here._____

_____
_____
_____
_____
_____
_____
_____
_____
_____
_____
_____

What behaviors are they specifically told to stop doing or to "put off"?_____

_____
_____
_____
_____
_____
_____
_____
_____
_____
_____
_____
_____

Philemon: A Study Guide for LIFE

Outline and Table of Contents

Background Information

AUTHOR: Paul, the apostle (Philemon 1:1).

DATE: About 61 or 62 AD. The letter was carried by Tychicus and Onesimus from Rome to Colossae along with the letter to the Colossian church (Colossians 4:7-9). The last chapter of the book of Acts mentions Paul's imprisonment during this time as being a house arrest in his own rented quarters.

THEME: On one of Paul's missionary journeys, he started a church in the home of a man named Philemon. Philemon had a slave named Onesimus who ran away and found Paul while he was under house arrest in Rome. Onesimus was a great help to Paul, for he was able to have the freedom that Paul was denied. It probably wasn't long before Paul led Onesimus to saving knowledge of Jesus Christ (Philemon 1:10). Onesimus was no longer just a run-away slave; now he was also Paul's brother in Christ.

Paul realized that he could not righteously keep Onesimus, but to make him return to Philemon would bring him punishment and could possibly result in his death. The resolution of this dilemma was the appeal from Paul that we have in this letter. Paul is sending him back to Philemon with an impassioned plea for him to forgive Onesimus and to accept him back into his household. He takes on Onesimus' debt and reminds Philemon of his own obligations to Paul and to the very Lord that Paul, Philemon and Onesimus now have in common.

Philemon – A Study Guide for LIFE

A-1   Paul's Salutation – Philemon 1:1-3

Philemon 1:1-3   *Paul, a prisoner of Christ Jesus, and Timothy our brother, To Philemon our beloved [brother] and fellow worker, 2 and to Apphia our sister, and to Archippus our fellow soldier, and to the church in your house: 3 Grace to you and peace from God our Father and the Lord Jesus Christ.*

FYI: **Archippus** (Gk. *Archippos*) -- *Horse-ruler, the master of the [war] horse.* The reference to a *fellow soldier* could be seen as a play on his name. He is also mentioned in Colossians 4:17.

Philemon (Gk. *one who kisses*) -- A resident of Colossae (Colossians 4:9) and a convert of Paul (Philemon 1:19). As a fellow worker, he was active in the church and had apparently worked alongside Paul.

Paul was in Rome but was under house arrest, as mentioned in Acts 28:16, 30-31.

This letter follows the standard format for letters; namely, it begins with a statement identifying *from whom* and *to whom* the letter was written, followed by a *blessing* on the recipient.

TQ: ** Who wrote the letter?_____
_____
** To whom was the letter written?_____
_____
** What is the blessing?_____
_____
** Paul was imprisoned in Rome by the Roman government. Why does he state that he is a prisoner of Christ Jesus?_____
_____
** Who is with Paul in Rome?_____
_____
** Where was the church that Philemon attended?_____
_____

A-2   Paul's Thanksgiving – Philemon 1:4-7

Philemon 1:4-6   *I thank my God always, making mention of you in my prayers, 5 because I hear of your love and of the faith which you have toward the Lord Jesus and to-*

ward all the saints; **6** *[and I pray] that the fellowship of your faith may become effective through the knowledge of every good thing which is in you for Christ's sake.*

TQ: ** Why does Paul mention Philemon in his prayers?_____

_____

** Where is Philemon's love directed?_____

_____

DQ: ** Analyze Paul's prayer and explain "the fellowship of your faith."_____

_____

** What would faith look like if it were to "become effective" ?_____

_____

** What is "the knowledge of every good thing which is in you"?_____

_____

** What would those "good things" be?_____

_____

** What does he mean, "for Christ's sake"?_____

_____

Philemon 1:7   *For I have come to have much joy and comfort in your love, because the hearts of the saints have been refreshed through you, brother.*

TQ: ** What had given Paul joy and comfort?_____

_____

DQ: ** How do you suppose Philemon had refreshed the hearts of the saints?_____

_____

A-3 Paul's Request – Philemon 1:8-11

Philemon 1:8-9   *Therefore, though I have enough confidence in Christ to order you [to do] what is proper,* **9** *yet for love's sake I rather appeal [to you]-- since I am such a person as Paul, the aged, and now also a prisoner of Christ Jesus--*

TQ: ** Paul made an *appeal* to Philemon instead of giving an *order.* What is the difference between the two approaches?_____

_____

** What was Paul's confidence based on?_____

_____

** What was his appeal based on?_____

_____

** How does Paul refer to himself?_____

_____

Philemon 1:10-11   *I appeal to you for my child Onesimus, whom I have begotten in my imprisonment,* **11** *who formerly was useless to you, but now is useful both to you and to me.*

FYI: **Onesimus** (Gk. *Onesimos*) – *Useful, profitable, helpful.* Note the play on his name in verse 11.
     This is Paul's first hint of the reason for this letter.

TQ: ** What does Paul mean by referring to Onesimus as "my child"?_____

_____

** When did Onesimus become Paul's child (and God's)?_____

_____

** What change had taken place in Onesimus since that time?

_____

_____

A-4 Paul's Explanation – Philemon 1:12-19

Philemon 1:12-14   *I have sent him back to you in person, that is, [sending] my very heart,* **13** *whom I wished to keep with me, so that on your behalf he might minister to me in my imprisonment for the gospel;* **14** *but without your consent I did not want to do anything, so that your goodness would not be, in effect, by compulsion but of your own free will.*

TQ: ** What did Paul say about Onesimus?_____

_____

** What did Paul really want to do with Onesimus?_____

_____

** Why didn't he do it?_____

_____

** Why didn't Paul use his authority to force Philemon to do the "right thing"?_____

_____

DQ: ** There is nothing in the Bible that speaks against slavery, but when a culture believes in and applies what the Bible teaches, then slavery is gradually eliminated. Review 1 Corinthians 7:20-24 in light of this passage and discuss what Paul says about slavery._____

** What does Paul's treatment of Onesimus tell us about his view of slave ownership in this situation?_____

** Would Paul be involved in freeing slaves today?_____

** Explain your thinking._____

Philemon 1:15-16   *For perhaps he was for this reason separated [from you] for a while, that you would have him back forever,* **16** *no longer as a slave, but more than a slave, a beloved brother, especially to me, but how much more to you, both in the flesh and in the Lord.*

TQ: ** Paul looked at the larger picture and used the spiritual benefit to Onesimus as the reason or benefit for his running away. What does he say?_____

** Describe the difference between a "slave" and a "beloved brother."

** Describe the difference between "in the flesh" and "in the Lord."_____

DQ: ** If Philemon ignores Paul's plea, Onesimus could be severely punished or even killed for running away. Why do you suppose Onesimus would be willing to go back to Philemon?_____

Philemon 1:17-19   *If then you regard me a partner, accept him as [you would] me.* **18** *But if he has wronged you in any way or owes you anything, charge that to my account;* **19** *I, Paul, am writing this with my own hand, I will repay it (not to mention to you that you owe to me even your own self as well).*

TQ: ** What is Paul asking for in this passage?_____

** Assuming that Onesimus had robbed Philemon, how could Philemon "charge" the theft to "Paul's account"?_____

** Paul is underwriting Onesimus' debt, but what does he "mention" that he "isn't mentioning"?_____

DQ: ** Why was Philemon indebted to Paul?_____

** Would you think that Onesimus' debt to Philemon would be less than, or greater than, Philemon's debt to Paul?_____

A-5 Paul's Conclusion – Philemon 1:20-25

Philemon 1:20-22 *Yes, brother, let me benefit from you in the Lord; refresh my heart in Christ. 21 Having confidence in your obedience, I write to you, since I know that you will do even more than what I say. 22 At the same time also prepare me a lodging, for I hope that through your prayers I will be given to you.*

TQ: ** How would Paul benefit from Philemon?_____

** What would refresh his heart in Christ?_____

** Clearly state how Paul expects Philemon to "be obedient."_____

** What two additional things does Paul subtly request for his own benefit?_____

DQ: ** Is one *obedient* to an appeal such as this, or is this appeal more than a request?_____

Philemon 1:23-24 *Epaphras, my fellow prisoner in Christ Jesus, greets you, 24 [as do] Mark, Aristarchus, Demas, Luke, my fellow workers.*

FYI: **Epaphras** ("lovely")
                 Mark ("a defense")
                 Aristarchus ("best ruler")
                 Demas ("governor of the people")
                 Luke ("light giving")

TQ: ** These are the names of Paul's companions in ministry. Detail the information that is known about them from the following references.
          ** **Epaphras**: Colossians 1:7, 4:12_____

          ** **Mark**: Acts 12:12, 25; 15:37-39; Colossians 4:10; 2 Thessalonians 4:11; 1 Peter 5:13_____

          ** **Aristarchus**: Acts 19:29, 27:2, Colossians 4:10_____

          ** **Demas**: Colossians 4:14, 2 Timothy 4:10_____

          ** **Luke**: Colossians 4:14, 2 Timothy 4:11_____

Philemon 1:25   *The grace of the Lord Jesus Christ be with your spirit.*

TQ: ** Evaluate Paul's letter and point out specific phrases where Paul demonstrated the graciousness of the Lord in his appeal.

DQ: ** We tend to say these words rather glibly and without a lot of meaning, but contemplate and describe the effect this blessing would have if you were to actually receive it in your life._____

          ** Would this blessing benefit you personally or would it primarily be for others?_____
          ** Explain your thoughts._____

RECAP: Write a brief summary of this letter and explain the background experience Paul had with both Onesimus and Philemon._____

_____

_____

_____

_____

_____

_____

What action did Paul expect of Onesimus?_____

_____

_____

_____

_____

What did he expect of Philemon?_____

_____

_____

_____

_____

Evaluate the psychology of Paul's approach in this letter._____

_____

_____

_____

_____

_____

Personal Notes_____

_____

_____

_____

_____

_____

_____

_____

_____

_____

Glossary of Terms

The terms below are used in these Study Guides for LIFE. The definitions and discussions provide additional details, information and references for students who want a fuller understanding of the terms than what is offered in the text.

Adoption as Sons: A Jewish son was trained as a child (Gk. *teknon,* a son by right of birth) of the family until he was fully qualified to operate the business of the father. At the time the father determined he was ready, trained and matured (probably around the age of 30), he "adopted him as a son" (Gk. *huios,* a mature son, one who bears the character and nature of his father) and made him an equal partner of the business. The term *Adoption As Sons* (Gk. *huiothesia*: Romans 8:15, 23, 9:4, Galatians 4:5, Ephesians 1:5) refers to a future event in the lives of believers when they are fully matured, fully trained and ready to be made a partner in the Family Business. (The "Family Business" will be ruling the nations of the earth with Christ.) A believer's *adoption as a son* will ultimately take place at his or her resurrection (Romans 8:23).   Believers are considered sons (*huios*) of God by faith (Galatians 3:26). Until our adoption as sons finally takes place we are considered a *teknon*-child (Romans 8:16-17, 1 John 3:2). Both men and women will receive the adoption as sons, it is not related to gender, culture or social status (Galatians 3:28). We are *huios*--mature sons--today to the extent we are being led by the Spirit of God (Romans 8:14). A child (*teknon*) is one born of God; a son (*huios*) is one taught of God. A child has God's nature; a son has God's character.

Believers are *born* into the family of God, *not adopted* (John 3:3-7; 1 Peter 1:3, 23; 1 John 2:29, 3:9, 5:1). Once born again, believers have a new Father (John 8:44, 1 John 3:1-2) and the training/maturing process that leads to our *adoption as sons* begins.

Body: Man is composed of body, soul and spirit. His *body* is that physical part of his being which allows him to function in a physical world. The body has 5 main functions:

NUTRITION: The assimilation of nutrients (food and drink, oxygen) for growth and the replacement of tissues;

REPRODUCTION, Sexuality, to provide for the continuation of the human species;

COMMUNICATION: The exchange of thoughts, messages, or information by verbal and nonverbal means (speech, gestures or writing);

DEFENSE: Protection against attack, danger or injury. Defense causes one to fight or take flight when in danger;

SENSING: (Sight, touch, smell, hearing, taste). Our senses enable us to receive input from the physical world.

Eternal Destinies: The following terms are likely to be involved in any discussion of our life after death:

Gehenna: The New Testament name for the place where the spirits of the _un_righteous dead are being temporarily kept until their final judgment. _Gehenna_ was the name of the garbage dump outside of Jerusalem where the garbage was kept burning. _Gehenna_ refers to the suffering state of the wicked reflective of the burning and rotting of that garbage. _Gehenna_ is always translated _"Hell"_ in NASB (Mark 9:45-46). Gehenna will be emptied just prior to the Great White Throne Judgment after the Millennium as its residents are resurrected, judged and sentenced to eternal punishment in the Lake of Fire.

Hades: The New Testament name for _Sheol._ In general, and in the Old Testament, _Hades_ refers to the realm of the dead without regard to their righteousness. However the New Testament reveals that _Hades_ was comprised of two areas, one for the unrighteous and another for the righteous (Luke 16:19-31). When _Hades_ is used more specifically, it refers to the area where the _un_righteous were kept, as distinct from _Abraham's bosom_ or _Paradise._ When _Paradise_ was relocated to _Heaven_ (Ephesians 4:8-10), _Hades_ became the sole location of the _un_righteous dead and is now synonymous with _Gehenna_ or _Hell. Hades_ and all it contains will ultimately be thrown into the _Lake of Fire_ (Revelation 20:14).

Heaven: The spiritual realm where God resides. Heaven is a spiritual place and is very real, but it is not located in the physical universe. Heaven contains God's throne (Revelation 4), innumerable angels (1 Peter 3:22, Revelation 5:11), and, since Christ's ascension, the spirits of the righteous dead have been located in _Heaven or Paradise_ (Hebrews 12:23, Revelation 7:9-17). It is from _Heaven_ that God exercises His oversight of planet earth. In the eternal age, God (and Heaven) will be physically relocated to the renewed earth to be with man as God originally intended (Genesis 3:8, Revelation 21:1-4).

Paul refers to the area of God's throne and _Paradise_ as the _Third Heaven._ The _first_ heaven refers to the earth's atmosphere, the second heaven is the region of the sun, moon and stars; and the Third heaven is God's spiritual realm (2 Corinthians 12:2-4). There are no direct references to the first or second heavens in the Bible, but they are implied in passages such as Psalm 19:1.

In the eternal age, Heaven will be located on earth, for God will reside there with His people (Revelation 21:3). It was never God's intention for believers to spend eternity in heaven. We will only be there until Christ brings us back to earth to be reunited with our physical bodies as we are resurrected or raptured (1 Thessalonians 3:13, 4:14-17). From then on we will reign as priests with Him on earth over the nations (Revelation 2:26-27, 20:6).

Hell: The English translation of *Gehenna*. The spirits of the unrighteous dead are currently kept in *Hell*, a temporary place of *torment*. (*Hell*, *Gehenna* and *Hades* are synonyms and refer to the same place.) Luke 16:19-31 describes the condition in Hell.

Lake of Fire: The final place of torment prepared for satan and his angels (Matthew 25:41). Those who follow satan will share his judgment. When unbelievers (those who follow satan's ways) die in this age, they (their spirits) go to a temporary place called Hades or Hell (Luke 16:23). At the final Great White Throne Judgment, Hades, and its inhabitants, will be thrown into the Lake of Fire (Revelation 20:13-15). Hades or Hell could be compared to a local jail; the Lake of Fire would be comparable to a penitentiary. Its name describes the eternal condition of the torment on those who are there (Mark 9:43-49). The intensity of this punishment will vary for each individual according to the offenses or deeds of the individual (Matthew 16:27, Revelation 20:11-12); but their location in the Lake of Fire indicates its severity, and duration of their punishment will be eternal, forever and ever. Life in the Lake of Fire is described as the second death, for it is eternal separation from God and all that is good.

It should be pointed out that God never "sends a person to hell." Throughout a person's life God presents him or her with opportunities to choose life (Deuteronomy 30:19, John 1:9, Romans 4:19). The choices a person makes according to their own free-will determine his or her eternal destiny, not God. God has no pleasure in anyone going to Hell or the Lake of Fire, but desires everyone to have life (Ezekiel 18:32, 33:11; 1 Timothy 2:4).

Paradise: An area of Heaven where the spirits of the righteous dead have lived since the ascension of Jesus. Christ took the spirits of the righteous dead from *Abraham's Bosom* to Heaven, where they now reside in a region called *Paradise* (Ephesians 4:8-10, 2 Corinthians 12:2-4). Luke 16:19-31 and Revelation 6:9-11 describes the spiritual bodies of people after the death of their physical bodies. They have bodies appropriate for the spiritual realm that mirror their physical bodies (tongues, eyes, fingers and bosoms are specifically mentioned. They have increased abilities in that they can see and communicate over great distances. They know other people, they feel, think, speak, remember, regret, wish and plan. They have thirst, emotions, expectations, limitations, a sense of justice and a desire for vengeance. They wear clothes and have all senses operating. Even though their physical bodies are dead, their life goes on.

Sheol: The place of the departed dead. The understanding of the

Old Testament saints was limited and *Sheol* was the general term they used for the place where all the spirits (NASB, *souls*) of the dead were located without regard to their righteousness (Job 17:13, Psalm 6:5, 89:48).

Flesh: Depending on the context, flesh is defined as:

    1) The soft part of the human body (Luke 24.39).

    2) The human body in total (2 John 1:7).

    3) All humanity (Luke 3:5).

    4) Individuals who follow the desires of their bodies or souls instead of their spirits (1 Corinthians 3:1-4, Ephesians 2:3, Galatians 5:19-21).

    5) Any activity that results from human effort (the body and soul) instead of the spirit. The desires of the flesh (the body and soul) are the opposite of the desires of the spirit (John 3:6, Romans 8:5-8, 2 Corinthians 11:18-33.)

Gehenna: See *Eternal Destinies.*

Hades: See *Eternal Destinies.*

Heaven: See *Eternal Destinies.*

Hell: See *Eternal Destinies.*

Kingdom: "*The governing influence of a king over his territory, impacting it with his personal will, purpose, and intent, producing a culture, values, morals, and lifestyle that reflect the king's desires and nature for his citizens.*" – Myles Munroe, Kingdom Principles.

    Jesus is our King (Mark 1:14-15, John 18:36) and He has come to establish His Kingdom in the lives of His people (Matthew 16:19, Colossians 1:13). Jesus will ultimately rule as King over the earth during the Millennium and the Eternal Kingdom (Revelation 19:15-16).

Life: There are three primary Greek words that are translated "life":

    1) *ZOE: God's life, eternal life.* This is the life we are given when we become Christians. References to our participation in *zoe* refer to the needs and comfort of our *spirits* (John 3:15-16, Romans 8:6, 2 Corinthians 5:4).

    2) *PSUCHE: Man's natural life, human life, the life of the soul;* therefore, references to *psuche* generally refer to the needs and comfort of the *soul* (Matthew 6:25-29, John 10:15, Matthew 10:39).

    3) *BIOS: Physical life.* References to *bios* generally refer to one's interests in lifestyle and livelihood or the needs and comfort of the *body* (Luke 8:14, 15:12 ["wealth", NASB]; 1Timothy 2:2, 4; 1 John 3:17 ["goods", NASB]).

Love: Love is difficult to define and is easily confused with lust or infatuation. God is love; therefore, love could be defined as Christ-like behavior (John

13:34-35 1 John 3:14, 4:20). It is a self-denying, non-emotional act that seeks the best for another person (1 Thessalonians 5:15). Love is behavior that reflects the total of all virtues with none being ignored; for instance, a husband who is kind, considerate and generous, but cheats on his wife, is not showing love. 1 Corinthians 13 describes love. God's moral law is based on love (Matthew 22:37).

The Greek language (the language of the original New Testament documents) uses different words for love:

1) *PHILEO (Philadelphia, Philanthropia)*—Human love, brotherly love, affection. (Matthew 6:5, 10:37)

2) *AGAPAO (Agape)*—God's self-sacrificing love for man. (John 13:34, 15:12-13) (Paul uses *agape* in this passage.)

3) *EROS*—Sexual love. This is a valid Greek word, but it is not used in the New Testament.

Mystery: A mystery in the New Testament is a truth that has been concealed in the past, but has now been revealed. Several concepts in the New Testament are referred to as mysteries:

--The hardening of Israel so the Gentiles could come into the Kingdom (Romans 11:26);

--Christ indwelling Gentile believers, giving them hope (Colossians 1:26-27);

--The inclusion of both the Gentiles and the Jews into one body (Ephesians 3:3-6);

--The gospel, or salvation through faith in Christ (Romans 16:25, 1 Corinthians 2:7-8, Ephesians 6:19);

--The resurrection and rapture of living saints (1 Corinthians 15:51-52);

--The Church (Ephesians 5:32).

Paradise: See *Eternal Destinies.*

Predestination: Reformed theology teaches that God in His sovereignty predestines every person to either heaven or hell. Arminianism teaches that the free will of man allows a person to choose the path that will lead to one or the other. The truth is between these two positions. God sovereignly chooses the path that leads to salvation and invites or calls mankind to exercise his free-will to follow it. As long as the man listens and responds to God, he is destined (or on the path that leads) to reach heaven or glorification. If he rejects God, he is destined, or on the path that will take him to hell. God, in His foreknowledge knows who will or won't accept His offer, but He extends His invitation to everyone (1 Timothy 2:3-4; John 3:17). Many verses reflect this balance, for example: Deuteronomy 30:19; Ezekiel 18.23; John 7:37; Acts 2:21, 39; Revelation 3:20, 22:17.

God has determined before the foundation of the world (*predesti-*

nated) that those who believe in Christ should be conformed to His likeness (Romans 8:29), and will receive an inheritance with Christ (Ephesians 1:5). God's predestination of His people includes all that His kind intentions have purposed for us (Romans 8:30, Ephesians 1:5).

Reconciliation: Being placed in friendship with God. As sinners we were God's enemies, but when we exercise faith in Christ, our sins are forgiven and we are born into God's family (Romans 5:10). Reconciliation begins with salvation, but through the process of sanctification, our thoughts, habits, attitudes and all our behaviors are brought in line (reconciled) with God's nature and character (1 Corinthians 5:20). Thus, reconciliation is the beginning point of our salvation, but it is also the goal of the life-long process of sanctification.

Redemption: A release obtained by paying a ransom. In the case of our salvation, we were lost under the penalty of our sins (Ezekiel 18:20). Christ's death paid that penalty in order to redeem us. The ransom was NOT paid to satan; it was the purchase price required by God and was paid to Him (Ephesians 1:7, Hebrews 9:12-15).

This price was the sacrifice that is known as *our propitiation*, the sacrifice that satisfies God's requirements. Animal sacrifices only *atoned* for man's sins; that is, only covered them over temporarily. Christ's death is the propitiation, the one sacrifice that God accepts as the price of redemption to forgive and totally remove the sins of man. God's forgiveness is given freely to those who believe and accept His sacrifice as the payment for their sins (Romans 3:25, 1 John 2:2).

Sanctification: Set apart (as a husband and wife are set apart or sanctified to each other); made holy or righteous. There are two aspects of sanctification:

1) IMPUTED or POSITIONAL. God imputes to us the righteousness of Christ in our salvation. When God considers us, He sees us in Christ with all of Christ's righteousness. This condition is realized when we believe in Christ and is the result of our justification (Romans 4:5).

2) PRACTICAL or PROGRESSIVE. Even though God sees us as righteous, man sees us as our behaviors dictate. A thief who receives salvation (and imputed righteousness or sanctification) may still go to jail for his crimes. The goal of salvation is to make us righteous both in position and in practice. God does this through the convicting work of the Holy Spirit which leads us toward Christ-likeness (Ephesians 4:13, 2 Corinthians 3:18). As we walk in obedience to His voice and the written Word, our practical sanctification will progressively conform us more and more to the righteousness that has been imputed to our accounts (Romans 6:19-22, 1 Thessalonians 4:7-8).

Sheol: See *Eternal Destinies*

Soul: Man is made aware of his existence by the work of his soul. The soul is the seat of his personality and is comprised of his:

MIND (reason, intellect, memory),

WILL (his ability to choose) and

EMOTIONS (feelings of affection and desire).

In this age, a person is a soul who lives in a body and has a spirit (1 Corinthians 15:45). The soul is responsible for the entire person and must humbly agree with the spirit in order to obey God. The way of the soul and the body ("flesh") is contrary to the way of the Spirit (Romans 8:4-8, 13; Galatians 5:16-17).

Spirit of Man: A human being is composed of body, soul and spirit. The spirit is that part which is eternal and through which God and a person communicate. God resides in the spirit of the believer through His Holy Spirit (1 Corinthians 3:16). The spirit of man has three functions:

INTUITION: The language God uses to speak to us. It is an inner sense of rightness, a "gut feeling", or a knowing that came without learning. Intuition is like the knowledge one has in night dreams when you "know" facts that aren't in evidence or are even contrary to the evidence that you see. We "know" these facts with our spirits, but process and understand them with our minds.

CONSCIENCE: The means by which God indicates His approval or disapproval of our actions. Conscience uses intuition to communicate this approval or disapproval. One may logically conclude that a course of action is correct (according to reason, or the mind), but know in his spirit that it is the wrong thing to do.

COMMUNION: The means by which we worship, pray and have fellowship with God. True worship is not done in either the body or the soul, but in the spirit (John 4:24, Matthew 6:7).

In most translations, *Spirit* (with a capital S) indicates God's Spirit. When used with a lower case *s*, *spirit* refers to man's spirit. This is a device used by the translators to clarify their understanding of the text: it is not part of the text in the original manuscripts. On occasion, the translators make a mistake, so read the context carefully and determine for yourself if *spirit* (or *Spirit*) refers to God or man's spirit.

Word: There are two Greek words that are normally translated "word"; *logos* and *rhema* in the New Testament.

LOGOS: depending on the context, *logos* has a broad range of meanings, It is a general word for speaking, but includes rational content. It is translated with such terms as: *word, speech, question, command, report, message, teaching, statement, assertion, subject matter,* and *message*. Christ is referred to as the *Logos* (John 1:1, 14). A short-hand meaning has developed in modern Christian circles whereby *logos* refers to the written word, or the Scriptures (1 Thessalonians 2:13). This is in contrast to a *rhema* word.

RHEMA: That which has been *stated* with a focus on the content, translated with terms such as; *saying, utterance, prediction, prophecy, command or direction, sermon, proclamation,* and *message*. In modern verbal short-hand *rhema* refers the words of God that are not written down but are spoken to our spirits (Romans 10:8, 17; Ephesians 6:17). Both words are important to a believer. We would read the Word (*logos*) of God in the Scriptures and listen for the intuitive impressions (*rhema*) by the Holy Spirit as He instructs and directs our lives (Luke 3:2).

This "short-hand" is a convenient distinction, but as you might surmise from the closeness of the definitions, it is not always adhered to by the New Testament writers. Examples of *rhema* where this distinction is ambiguous would be: Matthew 4:4, Romans 10:17, Ephesians 6:17, Hebrews 6:5, 1 Peter 1:25. Examples of *logos* where this distinction is not clear would be: Matthew 8:16, 13:19; Luke 5:1, Luke 22:61, 1 Corinthians 15:2.

World: A translation of the Greek word *"kosmos,"* meaning *order, something well arranged*. Depending on the context, it means:

1) The earth and/or those who live in it (Matthew 24:14, Romans 3:6), or

2) The orderly system of economics, politics and other systems under the control of satan, the god of this world (2 Corinthians 4:4). The world is in direct opposition to the kingdom of God (John 18:36, James 4:4) and directly appeals to the fleshly desires of the body and soul; namely, the lust of the flesh, the lust of the eyes and the boastful pride of life (1 John 2:16). Christians are in danger from being deceived and coming under the influence of these systems (Romans 12:2, Galatians 6:7). We live in the midst of this world, but are not to be a part of it (John 17:14-16, Romans 12:1-2, 2 Corinthians 6:14-18, Revelation 18:4).

The Author's Story

From *Sinner*, to *Servant*, to *Son*

I was born at a very early age on a snowy winter day in 1944, in Hood River, Oregon – long before it became the premier windsurfing area of the world. I joined two sisters who were four and five years old.

My father was a hardworking carpenter from the old school (Hard Knocks University). He had reached full adulthood by age three and thought I ought to follow in his footsteps. His view of a good day was to get up before breakfast and "work like you're killing snakes" until the sun went down.

My family owned a 10 acre pear and cherry orchard that was too small to be profitable, so Dad supplemented his income by doing carpentry work while my sisters and I did the daily work on the orchard.

I didn't like outdoor work. I enjoyed reading, daydreaming, and surprisingly, going to church. In an age before TV, I would ask Mom to turn on the radio so I could listen to the Sunday evening broadcast of a local church as I went to sleep.

One sermon illustration I remember from that era concerned the end of time. In the scene the preacher painted, all humanity was advancing toward the throne of God. They were assembled in three groups. The first group knew they were saved and would be accepted into heaven, so they were joyful, excited and hurrying to get in. The second group wasn't too sure, so they were hesitant and hanging back. The third and final group knew they were lost and would spend eternity in hell so they were moving as slowly as possible.

I saw myself in the second group. I was pretty sure I didn't belong in the first group, but I decided I would fake it and rush ahead to sneak into heaven with those that belonged there when my time came.

My interest in spiritual things was an indication that God was calling me to Himself, but I was too full of myself to respond, so I developed my own form of righteousness based on what I *didn't* do -- the form of religion that says, "I don't smoke, I don't chew, and I don't go with the girls who do."

There were several times in my teen years that I started to follow Jesus – God's way of righteousness. I started, but I didn't continue. Finally, when I was 19, God gave me one more chance.

I wasn't concerned about my sin (which was mostly self-righteousness), but I was very much aware I was not a Christian... and I was going to attend a Christian college (Seattle Pacific College, now a university)! I thought that wasn't right, so I prayed and said, "OK, Jesus, I hereby make You my Boss." It wasn't a profound beginning, but Jesus accepted my commitment and I officially and honestly joined "the first group" advancing toward the throne.

College life was OK, but my favorite classes were Bible and I couldn't get enough of them. So after my freshman year I transferred to Seattle Bible Training School (now Seattle Bible College) where I met and eventually married Diane, the girl of my dreams.

After four more years, we both graduated with our Bachelor degrees. What does one do with a degree in Theology? I had gone to school to study the Bible. I was called to follow Jesus. I had no interest in being a pastor or even doing full-time Christian work. What to do?

Well, how about mission work?

Diane had always been interested in being a missionary. Jesus was interested in missions. I was interested in both of them, so we tried to become missionaries. Over the next year and a half we tried several approaches to get to the mission field. Nothing happened. Nothing worked.

Hmmm. Let me think, I was once told the greatest needs on the mission field were for printers, teachers and carpenters, so....

Well, I had experience with my Dad as a carpenter and I was a Bible teacher in church, so I took a job as a printer for the Hood River News. Printing was boring, so during this time I served two terms as a part-time Hood River County Commissioner.

Politics wasn't boring, but it was worse than printing. So, after seven years as a printer, I took a job with United Telephone Company of the Northwest (now Sprint Telecommunications). I was hired to develop, write and analyze rates and tariffs which I then filed with the Public Utility Commissions in Oregon, Washington and California.

We continued to look forward to missionary work. By 1979 we brought some of the mission field home when we adopted a sibling group of four from Bombay, India. (Wow, am I getting old? It's now *Mumbai*.) Three boys and a girl, ages 10 to 14, joined our perfect American family. We already had one boy (Jeff, age 10) and one girl (Heather, age 8). First we were four, then, overnight, we were eight. Then six of us became teenagers, and two of us became very old.

Eventually, we passed that phase of our life. Our kids moved out and on to make their mark on the world. Then the Father opened up more of Himself to me. I woke up with the thought stirring in my heart, "I'm tired of studying the Bible. I want to know Jesus."

This wasn't a new thought and didn't occur in isolation, but it summarized what had been the unspoken desire of my heart for the past several years. The goal of my life was no longer to just *follow* Jesus, but to know Him, to know His ways and to make His ways mine.

Our life's journey has taken us to some amazing places since then. In 1994, when I was 50 years old, Diane and I finally became missionaries. We served four years in the Philippines under the auspices of Ministries To Christian Nationals (MCN).

Then we followed Jesus to Seattle where I served as Academic Dean at the Bible College we had graduated from 33 years earlier. Then He led me to pastor a group of senior citizens for a couple of years, and then on to Arizona where we retired.

Even in retirement, we followed Jesus and have gotten to know Him better. I've been on several mission trips teaching in conferences in India, Kenya, China and again in the Philippines. (Imagine that! Me, a farm boy from Oregon!) And it has been in retirement that the most profound change has taken place in my relationship with God.

It is said that our view of God, our heavenly Father, is often determined by our relationship with our earthly father. I respected my Dad, but as my older sister said at his memorial service, "He was a slave driver."

The way I related to God changed as my relationship with Him grew. When I was outside of His family, I related to Him as I had related to my earthly father, something like a demanding boss who insisted on perfection and demanded hard work at all times.

Then, when I entered His family (on His terms), Jesus became my Savior, and my relationship with God changed. I was no longer "the sinner," I then became "the servant" working for Jesus.

In my experience as God's servant, I didn't really relate to Him directly. Because I didn't hear the voice of His Spirit, I related to His Word, the Bible. I would get my direction from the Scriptures or others, but not from God. I did not realize, in any practical sense, that God is a present reality in our lives and speaks to us intuitively through our spirits.

I saw the shortcomings of just being God's servant when I was on a short-term mission trip to India. It was my "job" to pray for those who responded to the invitation for prayer at a city-wide crusade. There were five of us praying: there were thousands that responded to receive healing or a touch from God. I was utterly overwhelmed and began crying out to God for help to meet the incredible need I was seeing.

Over the next several days, I began to see that God was inviting me to a closer relationship with Him. I had become His servant years ago but found that it was not satisfying, either to me or to God. What God really wants is to be a loving Father to His family. He wanted me (and all His people) to become "a son" who is attentive to His heart, not just His Word.

I no longer see God as a demanding Father. I now see Him as He really is -- the loving Father who cares for me with all His heart, soul, mind and strength; just the way He wants me to love Him. He is the One I can safely trust regardless of circumstances.

I have experienced a life that greatly exceeded my highest expectations, but even if my life were to completely change, I know my Heavenly Father will use events and circumstances to accomplish ultimate good in my life.

There are now two absolutes in my life:

1) God's Word, the Bible. It is absolutely true, accurate and dependable in all matters to which it speaks. I depend on it completely; and

2) An ever-present Father Who loves me without reservation or condition. He is a Friend who walks and talks with me daily and is my ever-present Companion. I'm getting to know Him better, but an infinite God will be impossible to know fully even after we meet face to face. In spite of my failures and limitations, He is very gracious and is drawing me ever nearer to Himself.

He is also inviting you, as He did me. Will you join the first group, too, by making Jesus your Savior and Lord?

We all choose our destiny. What will yours be?

This life is just a temporary pit stop on the way to eternity, a sort of gestation period for our eternal destiny. Our bodies are just tents we live in for a season while we accomplish the ultimate purpose of this life – training to rule with Christ throughout all eternity.

If you'd like to discuss my story, this *Study Guide for LIFE* or your relationship with Christ, let's talk about it. Simply send an email note to StudyGuidesforLIFE@gmail.com.

I'd like to hear from you.

–James K. Crews, B-th, MA-th

71866972R00066

Made in the USA
Middletown, DE
30 April 2018